THE
UNSOUNDED
CENTRE

THE

UNSOUNDED

CENTRE

Jungian Studies in

American Romanticism

by Martin Bickman

The University of North Carolina Press

Chapel Hill

The author is grateful to the following publishers and individuals for permission to reprint excerpts from the works listed below:

"To Helen" reprinted by permission of the publishers from *Collected Works of Edgar Allan Poe*, edited by Thomas Ollive Mabbott, Cambridge, Mass.: The Belknap Press of Harvard University Press, Copyright © 1969 by the President and Fellows of Harvard College.

Journal entry, January 1850, reprinted by permission of the publishers from *The Journals and Miscellaneous Notebooks of Ralph Waldo Emerson*, Volume XI, edited by W. H. Gilman and A. W. Plumstead, Cambridge, Mass.: The Belknap Press of Harvard University Press, Copyright © 1975 by the President and Fellows of Harvard College.

Poems 115, 130, 153, 174, 199, 249, 271, 315, 412, 461, 508, 638, 712, 1053, 1056, 1425, 1445, 1558, 1580, 76, 98, 172, 324, 384, 405, 553, 632, 680, 827, 1091, 1129, 1400, and 1422 reprinted by permission of the publishers and the Trustees of Amherst College from *The Poems of Emily Dickinson*, edited by Thomas H. Johnson, Cambridge, Mass.: The Belknap Press of Harvard University Press, Copyright © 1951, 1955 by the President and Fellows of Harvard College.

Poems 306, 822, 1675, 153, and 1425: Copyright 1914, 1942 by Martha Dickinson Bianchi.

Poems 575, 461, 962, and 1053: Copyright 1929 by Martha Dickinson Bianchi. Copyright © 1957 by Mary L. Hampson.

Poems 281 and 474: Copyright 1935 by Martha Dickinson Bianchi. Copyright © 1963 by Mary L. Hampson.

Poems 832, 638 (5 lines), and 1564 (one line): Copyright 1931 by Martha Dickinson Bianchi. Copyright © 1960 by Alfred Leete Hampson.

Library of Congress Cataloging in Publication Data

Bickman, Martin, 1945–
The unsounded centre.

Bibliography: p.
Includes index.
1. American literature—19th century—History and criticism.   2. Romanticism—United States.
3. Jung, Carl Gustav, 1875–1961.   I. Title.
PS217.R6B5   810'.9'14   79-26042
ISBN 0-8078-1428-8

FOR LOUISE

Each Life Converges to some Centre—

Expressed—or still—

CONTENTS

Contents

ACKNOWLEDGMENTS

In often working away from the mainstream of criticism, I have come to particularly appreciate those who have given this project the benefit of their advice and interest: Robert Regan, Luanne Frank, Leo Marx, Frederick L. Morey, Harold Schechter, Barton Levi St. Armand, and Howard P. Vincent. I also thank my colleagues in the Department of English at the University of Colorado, and especially the two chairmen under whom I served, Paul Levitt and James Kincaid, for their receptivity and encouragement. Mentioning my indebtedness to my students is more than an obligatory gesture in this case: by frequently demonstrating to me that "conventional wisdom" is a contradiction in terms, they became true collaborators.

Poe Studies and the Department of English of the University of Texas at Arlington have allowed me to use in altered form material first presented in their publications. The University of Colorado Committee on Scholarly Publications has generously granted funds to aid in publication costs. Colleen Anderson performed with grace and precision under pressure in typing the final manuscript.

THE
UNSOUNDED
CENTRE

His experience inclines him to

behold the procession of facts you call the world,

as flowing perpetually outward from an

invisible, unsounded centre in himself,

centre alike of him and of them, and necessitating

him to regard all things as having a subjective

or relative existence, relative to that aforesaid

Unknown Centre of him.

Ralph Waldo Emerson,

"The Transcendentalist"

I.

MYTHODOLOGY:

THE SYMBOL IN JUNGIAN

THOUGHT AND AMERICAN

ROMANTICISM

This book is an approach to American Romanticism through Jungian psychology. Its wider implications, however, and the special character of its methodology will be missed if it is not read also as an approach to Jungian psychology through American Romanticism. Jung's psychological system is not taken as the basic and constant frame of reference, the single vantage point from which the terrain is seen. Rather, the psychology itself is viewed as another formulation, however powerful and useful, of the confluence of traditions that shaped American Romanticism. The literature does not serve merely as illustrative material for the psychology, but also illuminates the origins and nature of that psychology. This strategy helps to mitigate the main danger in confronting literature with psychology, reductionism, the error of simply transposing the former into the terms of the latter, or of giving the latter deterministic or at least causal priority over the former. Although it could be argued that any critical method is reductive,[1] psychological readings of literature have most often been charged with being distorted, procrustean, or peripheral. These problems can often be avoided by not taking the psychological scheme itself too absolutely or too concretistically, to break with those social scientists who, in Northrop Frye's words, "do not yet understand that their subjects, besides being sciences, are also the applied humanities, and that the myths and metaphors of literature inform them somewhat as mathematics informs the physical sciences."[2] Behind the Jungian approaches of this book lies an even deeper critical bias, that of practicality and pragmatism, of seeking to match method to material in original and yet productive ways.

In his voluminous writings, Jung himself takes several positions on the epistemological status of his methodology, but in his most lucid and candid moments he does not make the mistake that Frye describes. In *Psychological Types*, Jung writes:

> Every attempt at psychological explanation is, at bottom, the creation of a new myth. We merely translate one symbol into another symbol which is better suited to the existing constellation of our individual fate and that of humanity as a whole. Our science, too, is another of these figurative languages. Thus we simply create a new symbol for that same enigma which confronted all ages before us.[3]

Behind the refreshing relativism and modesty of this statement lurk several problems. If there is an ineluctable subjectivity in every symbol, inextricable at least in part from our individual and collective fates, does not any explanation become a mere mirror? Why keep creating new myths or symbols if "that same enigma" will remain? Does the psychological or literary interpreter face the dilemmas of both Sisyphus and Narcissus?

To begin to address these problems and to move directly into the kinds of alignments and interrelationships this study pursues, we can focus on the key word here, "symbol," and compare Jung's notion with that of Emerson, especially in his key 1844 essay "The Poet." This strategy tries not so much to make a case for direct historical influence as to show how the two writers can illuminate each other at crucial points. And because Emerson's writings are explicitly more symbolic and figurative, the juxtaposition will help us relate theory and practice.

In delineating the Jungian conception of the symbol, it is useful to return to the original Greek source and meaning, as set forth by the classicist James Coulter:

> *Symbolon*, as its etymology suggests, originally denoted a fragment—usually a half—of a whole object, such as a die, which could later be joined with (*symballein* means "to join") the other half in order that each of "two *xenoi* (i.e. 'guest-friends'), or any two contracting parties" might "have proof of the identity of the other." There is thus present in the word, from the very outset, two notions which later proved of great importance: that, first, of a suggestive incompleteness, i.e. the condition of being a single entity which yet hints at some preexisting whole or other larger entity of which it is a part, and, secondly, the necessity of some prior knowledge regarding the significance of the whole.[4]

Although the two notions are related, the "prior knowledge of the significance of the whole" will take on more importance in Chapter 3, whereas here we will focus on the "suggestive incompleteness" of the symbol. Leopold Stein draws further implications from the original Greek usage: "Symbols are thus tallies. When gripped together they make a whole containing the familiar (known) and the uncanny (literally unknown). . . . The symbol, the broken-off part is not a separate element but carries with it and points to, wherever it goes, the whole in which it participated as well as the situation in which it was broken in half."[5] The symbol, then, is tangible, concrete; but its very nature is to suggest something beyond itself, something not immediately present. Its suggestiveness, its indefiniteness, its resonances are not necessarily qualities inherent in the symbol itself but are related to its context, its origins, the way it penetrates a particular consciousness. The same object can be read semiotically, as a sign standing for something else equally definite and known, or symbolically, as Jung says, "as the best possible formulation of a relatively *unknown* thing, which for that reason cannot be more clearly or more characteristically represented."[6] As we have seen, Jung prefers "translate" over "explain" to stress the symbol's ultimate irreducibility and inexhaustibility. The symbol exists on a higher and more complete level of meaning than any and all analyses of it; it is the three-dimensional object of which any "reading" is a two-dimensional cross section.

The symbol not only encompasses the opposition of the known and the unknown, but can embrace all the dualities that at the same time beleaguer and energize our lives. It does so not by fusing these contrarieties indistinguishably together, but by presenting a deeper and broader perspective, from which they can be viewed as complementary rather than conflicting aspects of a more inclusive process, systoles and diastoles of a single rhythm. As Emerson writes: "By going one step farther back in thought, discordant opinions are reconciled by being seen to be two extremes of one principle" (2:308).[7] Jung sees this movement of thought, this step behind or beyond the plane of conflict itself, as fundamental to both the creation and the comprehension of the symbol: "What takes place between light and darkness, what unites the opposites, always has a share in both sides and can be judged just as well from the left as from the right, without our being any the wiser for it: all we do is open up the opposition again. The only thing that helps us here is the symbol: in accordance with its paradoxical nature it represents the 'third thing,' which in logic does not exist—*tertium non datur!*—but which in reality is the living truth."[8] The paradoxical nature of the symbol, then, can illuminate and express without oversimplifying what is often beyond the grasp of the intellect alone. Jung makes the point that the paradoxical symbol does more justice to the unknowable than clear rationality can, because the symbol does not deceive the mind into thinking it has actually captured that which is beyond it, making us mistake a part, a one-sided view, for the mysterious whole.[9]

For Jung, then, the symbol is not a distorted or displaced way of expressing something more elemental but perhaps too emotionally threatening. Nor is it an ingenious aesthetic device for expressing what could be said in simpler language. It is a way of knowing and of speaking that in some areas of human experience has more ontological validity than any other. As Jung writes of symbolically charged literature: "We would expect a strangeness of form and content, thoughts that can only be apprehended intuitively, a language pregnant with meanings, and images that are true symbols because they are the best possible expressions for something unknown—bridges thrown out towards an unseen shore."[10] This bridging, transitional function of the symbol is fundamental also to Emerson's view, as when he says in "The Poet": "I find that the fascination resides in the symbol. . . . A beauty not explicable is dearer than a beauty which we can see to the end of" (3:15–16). Elsewhere, Emerson writes: "The god or hero of the sculptor is always represented in a transition *from* that which is representable to the senses, *to* that which is not. . . . And of poetry the success is not attained when it lulls and satisfies, but when it astonishes and fires us with new endeavors after the unattainable" (2:180). One of the primary reasons for the existence of genius is that "a link was wanting between two craving parts of nature, and he was hurled into being as the bridge over that yawing need, the mediator betwixt two else unmarriageable facts" (1:207). For both Emerson and Jung, symbolic language always strains at the limits of language, of the already known and articulated. A man's speech should exceed his grasp, or what's a metaphor?

To follow this line of thought to its supralogical conclusion, any extensive exploration of this conception of the symbol would itself be symbolic, as indeed the initial quotation from Jung implies. It would use language that incorporates both the conscious and the unconscious, the logical and the intuitive. And a modern critic, Jeffrey Duncan, sees this as Emerson's basic strategy: "By means of language, the creation of symbolic or metaphorical structure, we render unconscious truths conscious."[11] Emerson both argues for and tries to enact himself the notion of speech and writing as "life passed through the fire of thought" (1:138). In *Nature*, he writes: "That which was unconscious truth, becomes, when interpreted and defined in an object, a part of the domain of knowledge" (1:35). We have to confront the paradox, then, that Emerson's exposition of the symbol may be a fuller and more effective articulation of the very concepts Jung has in mind, because the former's language is more resonant, transitional, metaphoric.

The opening of Emerson's "The Poet" may confirm this judgment. Emerson begins by lamenting that the symbol-making faculty has been isolated from the whole of life, producing people who "seem to have lost the perception of the instant dependence of form upon soul" (3:3). He then says: "We were put into our bodies, as fire is put into a pan to be carried about; but there is no accurate adjustment between the spirit and the organ, much less is the latter the germination of the former" (3:3). The analogy here, that the soul or spirit is to the body as fire is to a pan that contains it, is linked by its context in the essay to another relationship, that of content to form in a work of art. But though it is this very separation of content and form that Emerson attacks, his own simile presupposes and perpetuates both this duality and that between soul and body. For even if there were a more "accurate adjustment," fire and pan, content and form, spirit and organ would remain separate entities. The word "germination," though, does move us a little closer to reconciliation, containing the seeds of the metaphor of organicism that Emerson often uses to deal with dualisms that are hoped to be only apparent. This word is the only foreshadowing or transition Emerson gives us for the radical recasting of his imagery four sentences later: "For we are not pans and barrows, nor even porters of the fire and torch-bearers, but children of the fire, made of it, and only the same divinity transmuted and at two or three removes, when we know least about it" (3:4). The abruptness of this self-contradiction is mitigated to some extent by subtle shifts in the objects being negated or discarded as the sentence progresses. It moves from inanimate containers—"pans and barrows"—to active controllers—"porters"—to "torch-bearers," whose implements at once carry the fire and become it in the act of consummation. Pans and barrows enclose the fire, whereas the fire, by contrast, surrounds the torch. The metamorphosis is achieved completely through symbol, and if it is effective, it is because the reader recognizes that "children of the fire" captures that intense oneness of being that is at least potential within him or her. Significantly, the next sentence mentions "this hidden truth" that is presumably not accessible to those who read only on a literal or cognitive level.

This is only one example in the essay where Emerson realizes and vivifies his ideas so that form and content, image and thought become welded by the bright fire of the symbol, which at the same time creates shadows of suggestion and indefiniteness. As Emerson says in *Nature*: "A man conversing in earnest, if he watch his intellectual processes, will find that a material image more or less luminous arises in his mind, contemporaneous with every thought, which furnishes the vestment of the thought. Hence, good writing and brilliant discourse are perpetual allegories" (1:31). "The Poet," appropriately enough, is even more symbolic and imagistic than most of Emerson's other writings. Throughout, there are elaborated symbolic constructs used in place of, or in conjunction with, discursive exposition, such as "the three children of the Universe" section (3:6–7), where a series of corresponding triads is set forth, only to be seen more fully as aspects of the same ultimate unity, and the parabolic paragraph (3:22–24) on the propagation of poetry, spoken by a bard "using his freer speech" (3:24).

For present purposes, though, some more short examples will suffice. Emerson writes: "Being used as a type, a second wonderful value appears in the object, far better than its old value; as the carpenter's stretched cord, if you hold your ear close enough, is musical in the breeze" (3:13). The second part of this sentence not only says better what the first part says; it says more. The simile suggests not only that a cord can become a chord, but also what stances the mind must take to effect this transformation: a sensitivity to nuance, a closeness of perception, a willingness to view an object in its own physicality as well as for its intended function, the flexibility to convert what most would see as a visual phenomenon into an aural one, a playfulness and relaxation of propriety that enables one to put an ear next to a plumb line, an awareness of the extraordinary in the seemingly ordinary that helps one discover that not all Aeolian harps are marked and set off as such. That one could keep adding to this list of resonances, that each person's list would be somewhat different, but that these very differences would in turn strike off more resonances from other readers validates other statements within "The Poet," such as "Men have really got a new sense, and found within their world another world, or nest of worlds" (3:30). And here, too, the metaphor opens out and inwards as we envision new aspects of being nestling in the interstices and branches of the world as we previously and commonly knew it, aspects that, like fledgling birds, are ready to burst their shells, and soon fly off, like poems a few pages earlier "clad with wings . . . which carry them fast and far, and infix them irrecoverably into the hearts of men" (3:23). To return to the carpenter's line, we notice that within the verbal texture of the essay the music thus encountered is linked with the music of the spheres, which we hear "whenever we are so finely organized that we can penetrate into that region where the air is music" (3:8). The imagery here suggests an upward movement, but the word "penetrate" together with the simile of the plumb line presents an opposite descending movement. The ethereal here is linked with the mundane, suggesting the precarious but essential balance point the poet must occupy, "where Being passes into Appearance and Unity into Variety" (3:14).

Not only, then, is Emerson's conception of the symbol similar to that of Jung, but the former often gives us a richer and more direct experience of the entire process. As Jung himself says: "Concepts are coined and negotiable values; images are life."[12] But we should be less concerned with the weighing and comparing of the two kinds of achievement than with the ways they can reciprocally clarify and mutually strengthen each other. The conceptual often comes to our aid when we are mystified, confused, or eluded by the symbolic. Further, Jung's conceptualizations are based to a considerable extent on intense human interactions, and often have a certain explicatory power and another kind of immediacy at those very places where literary artists sometimes drift into the vague, esoteric, and involuted. As we will see, by provisionally and judiciously adopting Jung's viewpoints, we can apprehend what might at first appear to be distant metaphysical terms in Emerson, such as Unity and Variety, in ways that do speak more concretely and meaningfully to our conditions. This is not to try to make Emerson more "relevant" or more modern than he is, but rather to see him more clearly on his own terms— because often it is those very terms that for us may need more explanation and contextual elaboration.

However different their approaches may be, the symbol for both Emerson and Jung is the cutting edge of consciousness, the primary means of transposing the unknown into at least the suspected, the intuited, the embodied. But what may be one of the most sophisticated and advanced techniques of language and thought may also be the most primitive and basic. Emerson says: "As we go back in history, language becomes more picturesque, until its infancy, when it is all poetry; or all spiritual facts are represented by natural symbols" (1:29). Erich Neumann, a student of Jung who consolidated and extended his teacher's theories, sees the symbol-making process as inseparable from the initial process of becoming aware, from the way in which thought itself begins: "Symbols gather round the thing to be explained, understood, interpreted. The act of becoming conscious consists in the concentric grouping of symbols around the object, all circumscribing and describing the unknown from many sides. Each symbol lays bare another essential side of the object to be grasped, points to another facet of meaning. . . . Only the symbol group, compact of partly contradictory analogies, can make something unknown, and beyond the grasp of consciousness, more intelligible and more capable of becoming conscious."[13] An implication here helps us understand the perpetual need for the creation of new symbols: the basic enigma that Jung mentions, the unknown core of the self and the universe, cannot be apprehended directly, completely, and exhaustively. Although an individual symbol in itself may have a certain coherence and unity, it can never by itself completely fathom the unknown object or process it points toward. This individual symbol is, as we have presented it, a paradox, holding together opposites in a single construct, but its paradoxical nature becomes at once more forceful and more intelligible when grouped together in a myth or art work with other symbols in a creative tension.

Horace Bushnell, a contemporary of Emerson who did not share his theology but did take a similarly complex view of the nature of language and symbol, writes of the process in ways that converge with Neumann's description:

> We never come so near to a truly well-rounded view of any truth, as when it is offered paradoxically. . . . If we find the writer in hand moving with a free motion, and tied to no one symbol . . . if we find him multiplying antagonisms, offering cross views, and bringing us round the field to show us how it looks from different points, then we are to presume that he has some truth in hand which it becomes us to know. We are to pass round accordingly with him, take up all his symbols, catch a view of him here, and another there, use one thing to qualify and interpret another, and the other to shed light upon that, and, by a process of this kind, endeavor to comprehend his antagonisms, and settle into a comprehensive view of his meaning.[14]

We are forced, then, not to make a choice between opposites, but rather to take a more "com-prehensive" view that embraces both. Consistency is a hobgoblin not only because it suggests a mind at rest, but because it provides only a single narrowed peep into the mysteries of the self and the world, a peep condemned from the start to be partial and falsifying. The curved and fragmentary line, as Emerson suggests (12:11), may actually be the surest route in the mind's apprehension of itself and the world. When Walt Whitman writes that of his "real life" he knows "only a few hints, a few diffused faint clews and indirections" (8),[15] he is not as much pretending ignorance as perhaps claiming the deepest kind of understanding one can have on the subject. Emily Dickinson advises us to "tell all the Truth but tell it slant— / Success in Circuit lies" (1129).[16] The pun in the last word is well-taken; the truth told "slant" is in a sense a lie or a myth, but it might, paradoxically, be the most effective way both to discover and to express whatever the "Truth" is.

These notions can aid with some difficulties that Jung's theory of the symbol seems at first glance to pose. If indeed the symbol is the best possible expression, the clearest and most complete formulation of the elusive phenomenon to which it points, what can the interpreter explain or add? What is the purpose and method of any kind of analytic activity that deals with the symbol on a more discursive and conceptual level? In suggesting what the psychologist can do, Jung returns to an older sense of a currently fashionable word in literary theory: "The essence of hermeneutics, an art widely practiced in former times, consists in adding further analogies to the one already supplied by the symbol: in the first place subjective analogies produced at random by the patient, then objective analogies provided by the analyst out of his general knowledge. This procedure widens and enriches the initial symbol, and the final outcome is an infinitely complex and variegated picture. . . . Certain lines of psychological development then stand out that are at once individual and collective."[17] What Jung here calls hermeneutics is called by many analytical psychologists "amplification," where a dream or fantasy symbol is elucidated by material related to it in theme, imagery, or form either from the subject's own associations or from myths, stories, or other symbolic constructs of which the subject may be unaware. Although the former, more personal kind of amplification usually has a more obvious relevance, the latter can often develop wider perspectives and create insights that a too myopic look at the immediate data would preclude. Further, this more objective amplification can move the entire discussion to a universal plane, where more than the subject's own dreams and visions are illuminated.

We can return again to the initial quotation from Jung, and see that the creation or use of a new symbol does not make previous ones superfluous or obsolete. Rather, in ways hinted by Neumann and Bushnell, the new symbol provides us with one more point of triangulation—perhaps a crucial one—by which we can penetrate more deeply the enigma itself, or at least see more fully the contours and meanings of the prior symbols surrounding it. The present study uses Jungian psychology—despite its apparently conceptual and analytic nature—as the new symbol or set of symbols in a configuration that arises primarily from American Romanticism itself. In other words, not only does this study take as one of its central methods the hermeneutical amplification suggested and practiced by Jung, but the primary material for amplifying the American texts will be Jung's own symbology. On the one hand, Jungian psychology is obviously not identical with American Romanticism, and so there will be fruitful ways of multiplying antagonisms and offering cross views; but on the other, it is close enough, as the next two chapters argue, to avoid the kinds of force fits and distortions that some psychological analyses of literature create. Though amplification as a technique is certainly not new,[18] even to nonpsychological literary critics, this kind of extensive and relatively systematic application of it to American Romanticism may provide ways of encountering a literature that is always in danger of becoming too familiar to us.

Although this chapter has stressed so far the methodological innovation of the study, this claim has to be qualified by deep and pervasive debts to previous works about American literature that in various ways and degrees involve psychology, symbol, and myth. The most important are D. H. Lawrence's *Studies in Classic American Literature*, F. O. Matthiessen's *American Renaissance*, Henry Nash Smith's *Virgin Land*, Charles Feidelson's *Symbolism and American Literature*, R. W. B. Lewis's *The American Adam*, Leslie Fiedler's *Love and Death in the American Novel*, Leo Marx's *The Machine in the Garden*, Richard Slotkin's *Regeneration through Violence*, and Albert Gelpi's *The Tenth Muse*.[19] At least as influential as several of these books has been a series of articles on Poe by Barton Levi St. Armand.[20] Although most of these debts cannot be sorted out and made cogently explicit, it will help to place the present study in a critical context by discussing briefly, first, its relations to Feidelson's book and, then, some issues recently raised about what some have called the "myth and symbol" approach to American literature and culture.[21]

Although *Symbolism and American Literature* has not been the most powerful or anxiety-producing influence, this study shares some special affinities with Feidelson's seminal book, affinities that should be articulated even at the risk of seeming to make extravagant claims for this book by comparing it to such a work. Most obviously, both books have a conception of the symbol as a unifying element, a verbal bridge between dichotomies created by the rationalistic mind. Both works see this conception of the symbol and its various uses as central to the works of our mid-nineteenth-century writers. Both, further, are more interested in the sometimes obscured relations and similarities among these writers than in emphasizing or creating schisms, in separating them into opposing teams, such as optimists and pessimists or transcendentalists and antitranscendentalists. Both view Emerson as the central theorist and a major practitioner of American literature, a somewhat bold and advanced claim in Feidelson's work that has become virtually a critical truism by this time. Methodologically, both combine a modernist perspective with an interest in intellectual and cultural elements that historically precede and surround the texts, and try to blend each of these dual visions into an accurate and living stereopsis. And both books are, to use Feidelson's word, "speculative,"[22] but mainly to the end of a better practical criticism.

Having acknowledged all this may cause the present study to seem derivative or redundant, and so it is at least as important to point out some major differences. Feidelson rejects the category of Romanticism as too narrow, too subjective and personalistic, to apply to writers who turn to the literary medium as a way of transcending the gap between the self and the rest of the world. Although this study does not take a significantly divergent view of what these writers are attempting—the symbol in Jungian thought is also a means of uniting the personal with the collective, the individual with the universe—it does assume a wider and more inclusive conception of Romanticism itself, a conception that follows the work of Northrop Frye, M. H. Abrams, Harold Bloom, and others.[23] From this viewpoint, the achievement of the American writers is to be found not in how they go beyond Romanticism, but in how they deepen, broaden, and clarify its basic assumptions and traditions. Also, Feidelson's discussion stays primarily on the plane of aesthetics itself; he says of the American Renaissance writers "that the really vital common denominator is precisely their attitude toward their medium."[24] *Symbolism and American Literature* goes beyond the New Critical atmosphere of its time by explaining how and why, rather than simply assuming that, ambiguity, paradox, irony are positive values. But its explanations remain almost solely on the level of epistemological and cognitive argument. The stress on the vital link of awareness and exploitation of the artistic medium that Feidelson isolates often ignores or bypasses the emotional and psychological dynamics that accompany and underlie it. His thesis can account for some but not all of the passionate intensity with which these writers, including Emerson, wrote. This is not to criticize Feidelson for staying within the sharp yet broad focus he sets for himself, but to suggest how the two books can be read complementarily, as two different arcs curving around the same concerns and enigmas.

Some of the other books on the list above have been grouped together and subjected to intelligent but often overly polemical methodological critiques. Though the books in question have withstood these critiques, and though their authors are extremely capable of making any further defenses, the present study addresses some of the issues involved, because the same critiques could and perhaps will be made of this book. In other words, what follows is a preemptive maneuver, but one that will enable us to say more about the nature of the present approach in a positive and explanatory way. Bruce Kuklick is concerned with a problem he calls "presentism," the danger that some critics may "extract from an author what is significant for us, but lose the author's intentions."[25] Along this same line, Michael J. Colacurcio says that he can "see no way to avoid the conclusion (of E. D. Hirsch) that before we can know what a work 'reveals,' even in relation to the psyche of an individual writer, we have got to develop some adequately historical sense of what it could possibly have been intended to 'mean,' as a complex of intention designed rationally to communicate between an individual writer in history and an audience, also in history."[26] As one of his examples, he writes: "If we should want to know what the guilty fantasies of Goodman Brown tell us about Hawthorne's own inner life, we may well have to begin with his ideas about Puritanism generally and, in particular, about 'specter evidence.' "[27]

Taking for present purposes Colacurcio's own example, and taking his critical assumptions on their own terms, we can turn to the text of "Young Goodman Brown." Although the story is set in the Puritan community of Salem before the witchcraft trials, and although Hawthorne is concerned here with the phenomenon of Puritanism, the word itself does not appear, nor do any related words such as "Calvinism," "innate depravity," "specter evidence." What we do find are sentences like the following:

"My journey, as thou callest it, forth and back again, must needs be done 'twixt now and sunrise."

"Too far, too far!" exclaimed the goodman, unconsciously resuming his walk.

The fiend in his own shape is less hideous, than when he rages in the breast of man.[28]

Without launching into a detailed reading of the story, we can observe how Brown's invisible quotation marks around "journey" and the very rhythm of his sentence that links departure and return with night and day turn the action into an interpretation of itself; how Hawthorne concisely underscores the conflict between what we consciously say and what we unconsciously do; and how the real locus of anger, fear, and impulse is identified. The genius of the story is the way these psychological and symbolic concerns are linked to historical forces, all mutually illuminating one another. But if one has to assign priority on the basis of the text itself, the evidence suggests that the psychological issues are actually more historic, conscious, and intentional than the factors Colacurcio raises, which have to be abstracted and inferred both from the text and from other sources.

The point is not that a psychological or symbolic reading is in any absolute sense truer or better, but that using the very criteria upon which historicists like Colacurcio want to determine meaning, it is the more accurate one. "Young Goodman Brown" is explicitly about the workings of the unconscious and, to give another example, about the symbolic resonances of the serpent image, however implicitly or indirectly it may also be about Hawthorne's ideas on Puritanism and specter evidence. One confusion in the debate may be semantic: the "historical" meaning of a work does not necessarily have to do with the political and societal kinds of content that historians themselves usually deal with; the "conscious intention" of a work may deliberately and purposively have to do with the unconscious, as the second sentence quoted from the story indicates. To pursue and clarify this issue, we can look at the self-imposed limitations of Robert D. Richardson's *Myth and Literature in the American Renaissance*: "The present study . . . deliberately refrains from the use of twentieth-century myth theory, seeking rather to explore the concepts of myth that were available to mid-nineteenth-century writers, and limiting itself to discussion of conscious uses of myth in the literature of the American Renaissance."[29] While acknowledging the erudition and the general intelligence of this work, one has to question how real or useful the dichotomies implied here are. In attempting, for example, to maintain strict historical order and continuity, may we not be subverting it? For many of the important sources and impulses for twentieth-century myth theorists, as Richardson knows as well as anybody,[30] are precisely in the nineteenth-century theories of myths and their Romantic milieu. More importantly, how practical is it to restrict discussion of a work to the contemporaneous theories of myth and psychology that were available to an author before he or she began writing? For as this chapter stressed, the act of creating a literary work is an act of discovery; the making of a symbol, the joining of conscious and unconscious processes that can be put asunder only by oversimplification or distortion. A central assumption of this study is that these American Romantic writers were neither victims of unconscious impulses they themselves did not understand, nor bound to the psychological and mythographic theories that were then current. In the very process of writing their works, they advanced the exploration of the human psyche, an exploration that began before Freud and Jung and will continue in forms we can now only surmise.

It may seem strange that to appreciate fully this aspect of our American writers it is helpful to turn to a European who did his important work in the twentieth century and in another "discipline." But strangeness and circuitousness have not always been accompanied by failure. Heinrich Zimmer ends his splendid *Myths and Symbols in Indian Art and Civilization* by retelling and interpreting the Hassidic tale of Rabbi Eisik, who discovered the location of a treasure hidden in his own Cracow home only by making a long journey to Prague and listening to the dream of a palace guard. Zimmer writes: "Now the real treasure, the end of our misery and trials, is never far away; it is not to be sought in any distant region; it lies buried in the innermost recesses of our own home, that is to say, our own being. . . . But there is the odd and persistent fact that it is only after a faithful journey to a distant region, a foreign country, a strange land, that the meaning of the inner voice that is to guide our quest can be revealed to us."[31]

II.

VOYAGES OF

THE MIND'S RETURN:

THREE PARADIGMATIC

WORKS

We can begin the process of constellating around each other symbols and symbol systems by examining the convergences among Edgar Allan Poe's *Eureka*, Ralph Waldo Emerson's "Plato," and Walt Whitman's "Passage to India." The very differences in mode and style of these discourses underscore the basic underlying scheme of unity-division-reintegration that M. H. Abrams and Northrop Frye see as central to Romantic thought.[1] This initial series of cross views, however, is not an attempt to reduce all works of American Romanticism to a single structure or monomyth. The rationale behind presenting the congruence of the three works, and then aligning this congruence with Jung's theory of the development of consciousness, is to provide ways of dealing with other works that are more problematic and intractable.

In the works to be examined in later chapters we will be concerned less with delineating a paradigm and more with analyzing the complexities, ambivalences, and anxieties that accompany or impede its enactment. The paradigm can help us understand certain texts only to the extent to which it enters into a rigorous dialectic with the concrete ineluctabilities of language and form in these texts. This is not only because any paradigm is a heuristic, an abstraction, but because at least in the case of American literature the more formidable and fascinating texts are the less susceptible to schematic explanation. The very title of *Eureka*— "I have found it!"—suggests a resolution and lack of tension, as compared with other Poe works where the protagonist is still seeking, where "Discovery" is only a cryptic word daubed unconsciously on a sail (2:10).[2] Emerson's own struggles with the dualities of existence make more compelling reading than his depiction of Plato as an ideal figure who has no trouble reconciling the universe. And Whitman's grand processional, "Passage to India," does not touch the bewildering depths of "The Sleepers" or have the poignant immediacy of "Out of the Cradle Endlessly Rocking." So although this chapter isolates a central and pervasive pattern of thought, it does so only to create a tool for examining a much wider and richer range of literature than that which fits neatly into the pattern.

Poe's *Eureka*, ostensibly a cosmogony describing the origins, basic principles, and inexorable fate of the universe, has been used to describe the workings of Poe's fictions and poems.[3] Although this procedure has often been effective, there is the difficulty that *Eureka* was written in 1848, shortly before Poe's death and after virtually all the fiction and poetry were completed. Some critics finesse this problem by suggesting that the scheme was clear in Poe's mind all along, an idea which would seem to belie the title but which receives some support from the fact that sentences and longer passages in *Eureka* repeat almost verbatim sections from Poe's earlier work.[4] It may be more accurate and fruitful, however, to view *Eureka* as Daniel Hoffman and others have, as the ultimate Poe tale, as much a work of the imagination as "Ligeia" or "The Fall of the House of Usher."[5] Recalling Neumann's description of symbols grouping around themselves in the expansion of consciousness, we can suggest that Poe's tales and poems, so repetitive—perhaps obsessive—in their iteration of themes and images, led him finally to express certain discoveries with an almost schematic clarity. Rather than taking the tales and poems as embodiments of the already formed conceptions of *Eureka*, we can treat *Eureka* as a retrospective analysis of that literature.

Despite the meanderings and complications that often strike the reader as semantic prestidigitations, the basic design of *Eureka* is neat, abstract, and "sufficiently simple" (16:185). The only two characters, God and the rest of the universe, can be reduced—or exalted—to two even more general terms, attraction and repulsion: *"No other principles exist. All* phaenomena are referable to one, or to the other, or to both combined" (16:214). Further, these two terms can be seen as functions of an even more inclusive concept: *"the truth of Original Unity as the source—as the principle of the Universal Phaenomena"* (16:221). This discovery of unity may indeed seem anticlimactic, simplistic, and monotonous compared with the nuances and intricacies of Poe's other work, but it is an extension of this work rather than a negation of it. Like the two other main works to be examined in this chapter, the simplicity here resembles the primitive and unsophisticated but is not identical with it. What Neumann says about the phylogenetic development of symbols has a relevance to the individual artist:

> The earliest symbols to emerge are the simplest, which we usually designate as "abstract," e.g., the circle and the cross. They are closest to the nonvisual character of the "archetype *an sich*," and are to be understood as the pre-concrete and prepictorial form of the beginning, whose simplicity is elementary and not abstract. In the course of psychic development their schematic structure is filled more and more with sense content, but in the further development of consciousness they are progressively de-emotionalized and finally experienced as abstract signs of consciousness. The spirit aspect of the archetype seems to embrace the first depths and ultimate heights of man's conscious development, since it uses the same signs in the beginning as symbols for a still inarticulate multiplicity preceding form, and in the end for an abstract conceptuality succeeding form.[6]

To the extent that *Eureka* lacks the sensory and emotional content and the achievement of literary form of the other work, it disappoints us as readers, but it may aid us as critics. Its abstract and conceptual aspects, though, should not deter us from seeing the ways in which the work acts as a master symbol, as suggested by its subtitle, *A Prose Poem*. Although the prose does not usually have the compression and aural texture associated with other works given that name, it is poetry as Poe defines it in "The Poetic Principle": a bridge between the thoughts and things of time and those of eternity, between our world and the supernal. As a poem, it partakes more of Beauty, "an immortal instinct, deep within the spirit of man" (14:273), than of Truth, and so is dedicated "to those dreamers and those who put faith in dreams as the only realities . . . to these I present the composition as an Art-Product alone" (16:183). Along with ratiocination, then, *Eureka* as an art product makes extensive use of paradoxy as a way of knowing and speaking, as suggested in the following sentence: "The conditions here to be reconciled are difficult indeed:—we cannot even comprehend the possibility of their conciliation;—nevertheless, the apparent impossibility is brilliantly suggestive" (16:211). Later, Poe speaks of "conceptions such as *these*—unthoughtlike thoughts—soul-reveries rather than conclusions or even considerations of the intellect" (16:218–19).

The work begins with a kind of epistemological prologue, where the deductive method of Arries Tottle and the inductive method of Bacon, whom Poe, in one of his ham-fisted attempts at humor, calls "Hog," are seen respectively as creeping and crawling. Significantly included in this critique is an analysis of the contradictions in which Mill gets himself entangled when he makes the Aristotelian assertion that " 'Contradictions cannot *both* be true' " (16:194). The problem with both deduction and induction, however, is not so much their own limitations as their "proscription of all *other* roads to Truth than the two narrow and crooked paths . . . to which, in their ignorant perversity, they have dared to confine the Soul—the Soul which loves nothing so well as to soar in those regions of illimitable intuition" (16:195). Poe defines his primary method of intuition twice (16:197, 206) as "*the conviction arising from those inductions or deductions of which the processes are so shadowy as to escape our consciousness, elude our reason, or defy our capacity of expression*." This notion of intuition stresses the symbolic and poetic nature of the work: the results obviously can be and are articulated, but the processes from which they arise are initially unconscious. The method of the work, then, links the unknown with the known, the subliminal with the conscious.

As we move to the results themselves, we see that Poe posits at the beginning of creation a single unitary principle, "the primordial and irrelative *One*" (16:222), which then becomes diffused through the universe to form the world as we know it. Although this diffusion is presumably the result of the will of God, it is an unnatural and therefore impermanent state: "This constitution has been effected by *forcing* the originally and therefore normally *One* into the abnormal condition of *Many*" (16:207). The separate parts, then, maintain a disposition to return to this original unity, "a tendency ineradicable until satisfied" (16:207). To bring what is essentially a metaphysics into harmony with the physics of his time, Poe identifies the repulsive force countering this tendency as electricity, and the attractive force as gravity. The latter is also correlated with the body, the former with the soul: "The one is the material; the other the spiritual principle of the Universe" (16:214). Poe then scrutinizes and manipulates these terms so that the two become increasingly reciprocal and intertwined, suggesting that *"The Body and the Soul walk hand in hand"* (16:244).

Eventually, through a series of imagistic shifts similar to Emerson's transformation of fire imagery in "The Poet," the two become no longer opposing forces acting on matter but the constituents of the universe itself. As the universe reverts to its original state of harmony and unity, all dualities and contrarieties are resolved in a vortex of oxymoron. "When, on fulfillment of its purposes, then, Matter shall have returned into its original condition of *One* . . . shall have returned into absolute Unity,—it will then (to speak paradoxically for the moment) be Matter without Attraction and without Repulsion—in other words, again, *Matter no more*. In sinking into Unity, it will sink at once into that Nothingness which, to all Finite Perception, Unity must be—into that Material Nihility from which alone we can conceive it to have been evoked—to have been *created* by the Volition of God" (16:310–11).

Poe's scramble for words here seems to stem from an attempt to carry over the language of logical analysis—a language that was sufficient to depict a universe of multiplicity and distinction—to describe a unity that transcends opposites and differentiations. But he is aware here that he is speaking from the position of "Finite Perception," and his continuous restatements are designed to illustrate the limitations of this language. As he moves towards the final pages of *Eureka*, he adopts a language that is more intuitive, metaphoric, rhapsodic. Terming the former language "reductive" and the latter "expansive," Alan Golding describes Poe's linguistic strategy as follows: "The reductive moves the reader towards recognition of the irreducible semantic limitations of referential language, freeing him to approach analogically, with full awareness of its mystery, the realm of the unthinkable and unspeakable."[7] At the end of the work, Poe situates himself at the point we have seen Emerson describe as the best vantage for the poet, the transition between variety and unity, where both can be perceived in their true character and in their relation to each other. *Eureka* ends with a paean to the reentry of the many into the one. All beings, Poe writes, are

> conscious, first, of a proper identity; conscious, secondly
> and by faint indeterminate glimpses, of an identity with the
> Divine Being of whom we speak—of an identity with God.
> Of the two classes of consciousness, fancy that the former
> will grow weaker, the latter stronger, during the long suc-
> cession of ages which must elapse before these myriads of
> individual Intelligences become blended—when the bright
> stars become blended—into One. Think that the sense of
> individual identity will be gradually merged in the general
> consciousness—that Man, for example, ceasing impercep-
> tibly to feel himself Man, will at length attain that awfully
> triumphant epoch when he shall recognize his existence
> as that of Jehovah. In the meantime bear in mind that all
> is Life—Life within Life—the less within the greater,
> and all within the *Spirit Divine.* [16:314–15]

Despite the symmetry implied earlier in the text, this process is not exactly a mere return to the original state of the universe, but a reintegration at a higher level of being. The imagery of the bright stars blended into One, the consciousness on the part of the individual that he is potentially All, suggests a living, realized universe different from the monolithic particle the text began with. The notion of God functions increasingly as the ultimate symbol, the union of man and Jehovah, the body and the soul, death and rebirth. At the very beginning of this cosmogony the Word is made flesh—or at least matter—and at its end flesh is reunited and reformed into the Word. Toward the end of *Eureka* even this vision is widened, so that what seem beginning and end may be only phases in an endlessly repeated cycle: "Guiding our imaginations by the omniprevalent law of laws, the law of periodicity, are we not, indeed, more than justified in entertaining a belief—let us say, rather, in indulging a hope—that the processes we have here ventured to contemplate will be renewed forever, and forever, and forever; a novel Universe swelling into existence, and then subsiding into nothingness, at every throb of the Heart Divine?" (16:311).

A congruent pattern can be found in Emerson's "Plato," published in 1850 in *Representative Men.* Not only were both pieces written at about the same time, but both occupy an analogous position with respect to the other works of each writer. Both *Eureka* and "Plato" provide broad conceptual frameworks that subsume earlier, more specific, issues and tensions. The worksheets for "Plato" in Emerson's journals reveal a mind trying to align and relate all the antinomies at various levels of existence in a single elaborate schema.[8] Aside from external evidence, though, it is clear from the text itself that Emerson is trying to construct what he might call an algebra of consciousness (3:35): "Two cardinal facts lie forever at the base; the one, and the two.— 1. Unity, or Identity; and, 2. Variety. . . . Oneness and otherness. It is impossible to speak or to think without embracing both" (4:47–48). If these, then, are the two mutually interacting poles of thought, what should be the proper relation between them? Using

Plato as a living embodiment of the solution, Emerson sketches the ideal progression. After noting that "the first period of a nation, as of an individual, is the period of unconscious strength" (4:45), he points out that Plato had studied in Asia, where minds are inclined "to dwell in the conception of the fundamental Unity" (4:49): "Plato apprehended the cardinal facts. He could prostrate himself on the earth and cover his eyes whilst he adored that which cannot be numbered, or gauged, or known, or named: that of which every thing can be affirmed and denied. . . . No man ever more fully acknowledged the Ineffable. Having paid his homage, as for the human race, to the Illimitable, he then stood erect, and for the human race affirmed, 'And yet things are knowable!'—that is, the Asia in his mind was first heartily honored,—the ocean of love and power, before form, before will, before knowledge, the Same, the Good, the One" (4:61–62). Unity, then, precedes multiplicity both ontologically and in the development of human consciousness. Knowledge, intellect, or the ability to define and distinguish is in some ways a higher, more distinctly human faculty, yet it remains subsumed by Oneness. Unity not only is prior to multiplicity, but encompasses and transcends it.

Plato is a "balanced soul" (4:54, 55) because he always recognizes that "this Being exceeded the limits of intellect" (4:62). He keeps always before him the one and the many: "His argument and his sentence are self-poised and spherical. The two poles appear; yes, and become two hands, to grasp and appropriate their own" (4:55). As a philosopher, he understands how the poetic symbol is a way of knowing: "Thought seeks to know unity in unity; poetry to show it by variety; that is, always by an object or symbol" (4:56). And in the larger curve of his lifetime development, Plato's thought emerged from unity only to return to it: "Plato, lover of limits, loved the illimitable, saw the enlargement and nobility which come from truth itself and good itself, and attempted as if on the part of the human intellect, once for all to do it adequate homage—homage fit for the immense soul to receive, and yet homage becoming the intellect to render" (4:67–68). Emerson then puts in Plato's mouth the following: "'Our faculties run out into infinity, and return to us thence. We can define but a little way. . . . All things are symbolical; and what we call results are beginnings'" (4:68).

This elegant curve of consciousness, however, is not fully consonant with the details of Plato's biography, even as given briefly by Emerson himself at the beginning of the essay. Emerson tells us that Plato studied in Egypt relatively late in life (4:44) and that he only "perhaps" (4:42) traveled farther east. Emerson's Plato, though, is not entirely an ahistorical idealization, for the movement of his life does epitomize the view of Greek religious and intellectual development put forth by Friedrich Creuzer. Creuzer, a nineteenth-century German classicist who had a direct influence on Jung and at least an indirect one on Emerson, conceived also of the symbol as an indivisible image uniting the infinite with the finite, spirit with matter. Myth and legend, by contrast, as in Homeric Greece, tend to literalize the symbol and to overstress its solely human and active aspects. The great development of Greek philosophy was made possible by a return to the original powers of the symbol:

> Cultivated men, wearied by the wretched confusion into which the One and the Divine had been splintered, expressed healthy doubts. . . . They sought to bring the susceptible soul of the Greeks from the excitements of myths back to calmness, to bring the contemplation of the One and All back from the distractions of the Many. Symbols had been cast aside by the endless babble of old stories, and these masters now set symbols up again in their old dignity: the symbol that was primarily born from sculpture but which, bodied forth through words, through meaningful syllables, through the totality and compact vitality of its essence, could interpret the unity and inexpressibility of religion in a way legend could not.[9]

Creuzer goes on to say that these philosophers "look back not to the Hellenic fatherland but rather to the Orient and Egypt."[10]
Whatever the importance of Creuzerian ideas behind the larger

curve of Plato's development, the smaller epicycles within that curve, the continual and instantaneous movements between the One and the Many, are particularly Emersonian. In *Eureka* what was first presented as the central movement of the universe— diffusion from the One and then return—is from a larger perspective seen to be one small heartbeat of an even vaster cosmic cycle. In "Plato," a seemingly opposite but actually complementary process occurs: Plato's grand development, from the absorption of the Asian apprehension of unity to the European capacity for defining and dividing, which in turn leads to a fuller appreciation of the unity underlying these divisions, is reflected in each act of apprehension: "The wonderful synthesis so familiar in nature; the upper and the under side of the medal of Jove; the union of impossibilities, which reappears in every object; its real and its ideal power,—was now also transferred entire to the consciousness of man" (4:54). As Emerson writes elsewhere, "The entire system of things gets represented in every particle" (2:97), and the value of this representative man is that he "turns incessantly the obverse and the reverse of the medal of Jove" (4:56). It is this representativeness that makes what is actual and realized in Plato potential to everyone. As Emerson writes in "The Over-Soul": "We live in succession, in division, in parts, in particles. Meantime within man is the soul of the whole; the wise silence; the universal beauty, to which every part and particle is equally related; the eternal *one*. And this deep power in which we exist and whose beatitude is all accessible to us, is not only self-sufficing and perfect in every hour, but the act of seeing and the thing seen, the seer and the spectacle, the subject and the object, are one" (2:269).

Though Poe's vision in *Eureka* seems to stress the cosmic sweep of time and space and Emerson's congruent vision the individual human consciousness, both seek a dialectic for relating one to the other. In Whitman's "Passage to India" the ground of that dialectic, the locus of reconciliation, is the movement of human history. This is a late poem, published in 1871, and although there is wisdom to the growing critical consensus that the "real" Whitman, the poet of genuine force and mastery, is to be found in the first three *Leaves of Grass* (1855, 1856, and 1860), the later editions cannot be ignored for a full understanding of the work. For as in "As They Draw to a Close," published the same year as "Passage to India," Whitman often takes as his explicit theme "what underlies the precedent songs—of my aims in them" (501). This increasingly interpretative and self-reflexive interest can be seen just from the titles of other late poems—"These Carols," "My Legacy," "You Lingering Sparse Leaves of Me," "L. of G.'s Purport." At least as significant are his rearrangements and re-groupings, to clarify and to strike new facets on earlier poems through juxtaposition. "The Sleepers," for example, published in the first edition of *Leaves of Grass*, is placed toward the end of the ninth and last edition, directly after "Passage to India" and "Prayer of Columbus." Although one critic sees this as "one of the most clumsy of his arrangements,"[11] the strategy gives more resonance and meaning to lines in the earlier, more elusive poem, such as "I descend my western course, my sinews are flaccid, / Perfume and youth course through me and I am their wake" (427), and "They [the sleepers] flow hand in hand over the whole earth from east to west as they lie unclothed, / The Asiatic and African are hand in hand, the European and American are hand in hand" (432).

As with *Eureka* and "Plato," then, "Passage to India" can be viewed as an attempt—to use Whitman's own word—to "eclair-cise" (412) the earlier work, to give some order and perspective to it, to answer some of the questions it raises. The most dramatic example is the poem's relation to a haunting lyric first published in 1860:

> Facing west from California's shores,
> Inquiring, tireless, seeking what is yet unfound,
> I, a child, very old, over waves, towards the house of
>   maternity, the land of migrations, look afar,
> Look off the shores of my Western sea, the circle
>   almost circled;
> For starting westward from Hindustan, from the vales
>   of Kashmere,

From Asia, from the north, from the God, the sage, and
  the hero,
From the south, from the flowery peninsulas and the
  spice islands,
Long having wander'd since, round the earth having
  wander'd,
Now I face home again, very pleas'd and joyous,
(But where is what I started for so long ago?
And why is it yet unfound?)   [110–11]

The oxymoron "a child, very old" suggests that the speaker here
is another representative man, perhaps emblematic of primitive,
presumably Asian man transforming himself into civilized European man who has now come back almost full circle, having made
a journey of conquest and discovery through an entire continent
of wilderness. This hint of restored innocence is emphasized by
the poem's context: its placement in the "Children of Adam" section, the first line of which is "To the garden the world anew
ascending" (90), followed by the last poem in the sequence, "As
Adam Early in the Morning." But the notion of a new Adam is
undercut by the implication that the speaker is a child not only
through innocence, but through ignorance and incompleteness.
He stands on the verge of some new revelation, but also finds himself facing "home again" with something still "unfound," something lost in the past, inarticulable but felt.
  In "Passage to India," this single speaker is transformed into
the entire race, the anxiety increased, and the two final questions
expanded into an urgent litany.

Down from the gardens of Asia descending radiating,
Adam and Eve appear, then their myriad progeny after them,
Wandering, yearning, curious, with restless explorations,
With questionings, baffled, formless, feverish, with
  never-happy hearts,
With that sad incessant refrain, *Wherefore unsatisfied soul?*
  and *Whither O mocking life?*   [415]

This time, however, there are answers that the rest of the poem provides. "The circle almost circled" has by 1871 become the "rondure of the world at last accomplish'd" (414) through three technological developments—the completion of the transcontinental railroad in America, the laying of the Atlantic and Pacific cables, and the opening of the Suez Canal. These physical accomplishments, however, are only a necessary prelude to the great spiritual fulfillment that the searchers are pursuing so restlessly and yet so unconsciously. For the passage to India can only now be seen for what it was, a "passage to more than India" (420):

> Passage indeed O soul to primal thought,
> Not lands and seas alone, thy own clear freshness,
> The young maturity of brood and bloom,
> To realms of budding bibles.
>
> O soul, repressless, I with thee and thou with me,
> Thy circumnavigation of the world begin,
> Of man, the voyage of his mind's return,
> To reason's early paradise,
> Back, back to wisdom's birth, to innocent intuitions,
> Again with fair creation.   [418]

Just as Asia stood for Emerson for the unknown and unknowable, for the beginning and basis of human consciousness, Whitman's Asia is a land of "primal thought," specifically identified with the original site of the Garden of Eden. It is a time as much as a place, and a movement of mind more than both:

> The Past—the dark unfathom'd retrospect!
> The teeming gulf—the sleepers and the shadows!
> The past—the infinite greatness of the past!   [411]

But as section 7 (quoted above) suggests, no headlong regression into this abyss is proposed, but a reunion with it on a higher level of consciousness: "the retrospect brought forward," "the past lit up again" (416). We will not merely return to "the myths Asiatic, the primitive fables" (412); we will illuminate them with what we have learned in the process. As in the last paragraph of *Eureka*, an apocalypse is delineated in which all that was once separate shall be rejoined; all that was diffused, reunited:

> All affection shall be fully responded to, the secret
>   shall be told,
> All these separations and gaps shall be taken up and hook'd
>   and link'd together,
> The whole earth, this cold, impassive, voiceless earth,
>   shall be completely justified . . .
> Nature and Man shall be disjoin'd and diffused no more.
>   [415–16]

A single but prodigious sentence that Whitman wrote in a meditation on Carlyle serves as both a gloss on and an enactment of this vision.

> According to Hegel the whole earth, (an old nucleus-
> thought, as in the Vedas, and no doubt before, but never
> hitherto brought so absolutely to the front, fully surcharged
> with modern scientism and facts, and made the sole entrance
> to each and all,) with its infinite variety, the past, the sur-
> roundings of to-day, or what may happen in the future, the
> contrarieties of material with spiritual, and of natural with
> artificial, are all, to the eye of the *ensemblist*, but neces-
> sary sides and unfolding, different steps or links, in the
> endless process of Creative thought, which, amid number-
> less apparent failures and contradictions, is held together
> by central and never-broken unity—not contradictions
> or failures at all, but radiations of one consistent and eter-
> nal purpose; the whole mass of everything steadily, uner-
> ringly tending and flowing toward the permanent *utile*
> and *morale*, as rivers to oceans.[12]

This idea, Whitman emphasizes, is not uniquely new, but present as a core in the earliest existing religious scriptures (those of

India) and even in the prehistory before this, and yet it is put squarely before the scrutiny of consciousness, made centrally obvious, when buttressed by "modern scientism and facts." Apparent dualities and contrasts become smoothed out or swirled away by the sweep of Whitman's syntax. The final metaphor, as conventional as it is, points to an important imagistic bridge between Emerson's Asia of the mind and Whitman's Asia of "aged fierce enigmas" (420): both of these "lands" metamorphose into oceans. Emerson says of Plato that "the Asia in his mind was first heartily honored,—the ocean of love and power" (4:62). In section 9 of "Passage to India," Asia becomes less a fixed destination than an ocean for another kind of voyage:

> O soul, voyagest thou indeed on voyages like those?
> Disportest thou on waters such as those?
> Soundest below the Sanscrit and the Vedas?   [420]

This vision of Asia as a realm of beginnings, completions, and yet new beginnings has acquired tremendous force in our culture, but its roots, as we have seen, are deep in early American Romantic thought.[13] Thoreau, after describing how the ancient writings of India have a perennial freshness and kinship with nature—a notion echoed in Whitman's phrase "budding bibles" (418)—writes in a sentence that anticipates in microcosm "Passage to India" that "there is an orientalism in the most restless pioneer, and the farthest west is but the farthest east."[14] The narrator of Melville's *Mardi* also gives emphatic expression to this spiritual manifest destiny: "West, West! West, West! Whitherward point Hope and prophet fingers. . . . Oh boundless boundary! Eternal goal!"[15]

More central, however, than the image of westward movement back to the Orient is the basic homology of thought. All three works display a dialectical and in some sense circular dynamic, from harmony and unity, to rifts and diffusions, back toward reunion. This movement is epitomized in an entry in Emerson's journals, where three eras of history are distinguished:

1. *the Greek*; when men deified nature; Jove was in the air, Neptune in the sea, Pluto in the earth, Naiads in the fountains, dryads in the woods, oreads on the mountain; happy beautiful beatitude of nature.

2. *the Christian*; when the Soul became pronounced, and craved a heaven out of nature & above it,—looking on nature now as evil,—the world was a mere stage & school, a snare, and the powers that ruled here were devils hostile to the soul.

   and now lastly,

3. *the Modern*; when the too idealistic tendencies of the Christian period running into the diseases of cant, monachism, and a church, demonstrating the impossibility of Christianity, have forced men to retrace their steps, & rally again on Nature; but now the tendency is to marry mind to nature. . . .[16]

Here, as in the three longer works examined, more than a simple return to a previous stage is envisioned. The third stage, with its marital imagery, suggests a more mature and productive harmony between the mind and nature than the first, where man's deification of nature may have led him to undervalue his own powers. Rather than a circle, then, a better visual metaphor may be the one proposed by Clifford Pyncheon in Hawthorne's *The House of the Seven Gables*: "All human progress is in a circle; or, to use a more accurate and beautiful figure, in an ascending spiral curve. While we fancy ourselves going straight forward and attaining, at every step, an entirely new position of affairs, we do actually return to something long ago tried and abandoned, but which we now find etherealized, refined, and perfected to its ideal."[17] Indeed, as we trace a modern version of the paradigm in the next chapter and point out elements of its long foreground, we will find ourselves following such a curved spiral, culminating not in an ideal, but perhaps in a form "better suited to the existing constellation of our individual fate."

III.

ONE'S SELF I SING:

INDIVIDUATION AND

INTROJECTION

Individuation, Jung's theory of the development of consciousness, will add a different but congruent and complementary dimension to the paradigm, making it a more effective explicatory tool. Jung's work tends to be more systematic and conceptual, and therefore less resonant and symbolic, than the texts of American Romanticism, although the difference is more one of degree than of direct opposition. But what may be superfluous for the artist is often helpful for the critic, who must speak on a more analytic and rigorous level even when dealing with the numinous and the problematic. As in physics, the encounter with increasing strangeness and complexity does not prove the uselessness of models, but rather the need for more sophisticated, responsive, and flexible ones.

There are two related reasons why this configuration of Jung's theory with the works already discussed deepens and opens out the paradigm in ways that are neither arbitrary nor reductive. First, the theory is structurally analogous to the pattern of unity-division-reintegration we have just examined in American Romanticism; it arises from many of the same historical contexts and cultural conditions and shares many of the same basic assumptions. Secondly, it extends and fulfills a tendency intrinsic in

American Romanticism—that of introjection, of regarding philosophical and cosmological concepts as important primarily for what they reveal about the human mind itself. Jungian psychology completes the movement of American Romanticism to turn metaphysics into a phenomenology of consciousness. The most striking activity in American Romanticism is that of the psyche becoming aware of itself, of the imagination exploring those areas where ideas are felt as well as thought, and where spiritual aspirations and sexual desires are discovered to spring from the same inner dynamics. Both of these reasons will be developed in detail after Jung's theory of the growth of the psyche is set forth.

In Jung's thought, the individual psyche begins in a state of complete undifferentiated unconsciousness, a primordial wholeness that exists prior to and encompasses all opposites. This state corresponds to Poe's absolute and irrelative One, Emerson's Asia of the mind, and Whitman's dark, unfathomed retrospect. Out of this realm, what Jung calls the "ego" emerges, a psychic complex that serves as the center of consciousness, a core around which a personal identity is constructed. As the ego grows and develops, it tends to separate itself from the rest of the psyche, setting up barriers between consciousness and what remains and what becomes unconscious. This process is accompanied by the creation of other dualities, such as inner/outer, subject/object, light/darkness, masculine/feminine. Although this development is necessary for functioning in what we call everyday reality, for establishing a life and a living, it creates an imbalance in the "self," the entire psychic unit, and leaves a person divided, with only a fragment of his or her potential realized.

Later in life, this unrealized potential beckons toward a rejoining of the ego with the rest of the self in a fuller integration of personality. The ego comes to recognize that it is not an autonomous entity, but part of a larger unity, within which it must help establish a working harmony. As the ego turns inward to confront the entire psyche, it enacts the Emersonian paradox, most succinctly expressed in the first paragraph of "Self-Reliance," that the deeper one goes into oneself, the closer one comes to the universal and the collective: "Speak your latent conviction, and it shall be the universal sense" (2:45). For Jung, the unconscious is not merely what we have personally experienced and then suppressed or repressed, but a world of unrealized dispositions and potentialities, of aspects of being we usually consider sub- or suprahuman.

An important assumption of Jungian thought is that the psyche is a self-balancing, self-correcting system, in ways that have been compared to Emerson's notion of compensation.[1] Even if the ego does not consciously strive for wholeness, it may find reunion thrust upon it. It is particularly true for Jung that, as Lancelot Law Whyte has said in general, "the discovery of the unconscious is the recognition of a Goethean order, as much as of a Freudian disorder, in the depths of the mind."[2] This organic, almost teleological vision of the development of the psyche can be seen in the following passage from Jung: "The ego-conscious personality is only a part of the whole man, and its life does not yet represent his total life. The more he is merely 'I,' the more he splits himself off from the collective man, of whom he is also a part, and may even find himself in opposition to him. But since everything living strives for wholeness, the inevitable one-sidedness of our conscious life is continually being corrected and compensated by the universal human being in us, whose goal is the ultimate integration of conscious and unconscious, or better, the assimilation of the ego to a wider personality."[3]

The entire movement, then, of psychic development resembles our ascending spiral curve or, to use another figure, the parabolic arc of a projectile through which, as Edward C. Whitmont describes it, "we move from an unknown and unknowable source of being to separate existence through the illusion of ego permanence and the supremacy of ego-will and then turn back to the aboriginal source, carrying with us the fruits of conscious awareness that we have gained while we traveled the trajectory of the curve."[4] To vary the analogy again, we can view these three phases as corresponding to the three kinds of wholes that Proclus posits: "the first, anterior to the parts; the second, composed of the parts; the third, knitting into one stuff the parts and the whole."[5]

Although the term "individuation" is often applied to the entire process, it more precisely refers to this last phase of reunion and integration. This more specific use, as opposed to what has become a common meaning, refers less to becoming a distinct and separate person than to becoming an in-dividual, an undivided whole. Emerson goes back to this root meaning when he writes: "When the individual is not *individual*, but is dual . . . what concert can be?" (3:266). Similarly, Poe emphasizes this meaning when he writes of the initial and basic unity of the universe as "a particle absolutely unique, individual, undivided" (16:207).[6]

To add yet another metaphor for the process of individuation, we can turn to what Jung describes as a Copernican revolution in the psyche, where the ego realizes that it is not the center of its universe: "Sensing the self as something irrational, as an indefinable existent, to which the ego is neither opposed nor subjected, but merely attached, and about which it revolves very much as the earth revolves around the sun—thus we come to the goal of individuation."[7] Further, Jung's description of the felt experience of individuation here—"The individuated ego senses itself as the object of an unknown and supraordinate subject"[8]—coincides with the ending of *Eureka*, where "the sense of individual identity will be gradually merged in the general consciousness" (16:314). This experience is given more emotional texture—both from the attendant fears and from the attendant exhilarations—in a note Poe inscribed at the end of his own first edition of *Eureka*: "The pain of the consideration that we shall lose our individual identity ceases at once when we further reflect that the process, as above described, is neither more nor less than that of the absorption, by each individual intelligence, of all other intelligences (that is, of the Universe) into its own. That God may be all in all, each must become God."[9]

Toward the beginning of *Eureka*, Poe quotes the Baron de Bielfeld to the effect that " 'in order to comprehend what he is, we should have to be God ourselves' " (16:205). We have seen that Poe takes this as an invitation rather than as a limitation, but without falling into hubris or solipsism. In general, the One, or God, can productively be equated with the self in Jung's terms, if not always explicitly as in *Eureka,* then at least operationally in the dynamics of a work of literature. William James has written that although monism is emotionally and spiritually attractive, historically it has "kept itself vague and mystical as regards the ultimate principle of unity."[10] Jungian psychology provides us with a definite, although not necessarily exclusive, locus for this ultimate principle, the psyche itself: "What at first looks like an abstract idea stands in reality for something that exists and can be experienced, that demonstrates its *a priori* presence spontaneously. . . . the self, on account of its empirical peculiarities, proves to be the *eidos* behind the supreme ideas of unity and totality that are inherent in all monotheistic and monistic systems."[11]

Although this stance may seem aggressively agnostic, it is more accurate and helpful to view it as an extreme extension of the Protestant emphasis on direct experience as a basis for religious belief, an emphasis that takes on radical importance in American Romanticism. The main thrust of this strategy is not to negate the religious experience, but in some ways to authenticate and validate it. We can return to William James as a central link between Jung and the American Romantics. James, whose Swedenborgian father was a friend of Emerson, was also a psychologist and the central figure in philosophical pragmatism. Toward the end of his extensive book *The Varieties of Religious Experience,* James writes:

> Let me then propose, as an hypothesis, that whatever it
> may be on its *farther* side, the 'more' with which in religious
> experience we feel ourselves connected is on its *hither* side
> the subconscious continuation of our conscious life. . . . the
> theologian's contention that the religious man is moved by
> an external power is vindicated, for it is one of the pecu-
> liarities of invasions from the subconscious region to take
> on objective appearances, and to suggest to the Subject an
> external control. In the religious life the control is felt as
> 'higher'; but since on our hypothesis it is primarily the
> higher faculties of our own hidden mind which are control-

ling, the sense of union with the power beyond us is a sense of something, not merely apparently, but literally true.[12]

Jung, however, is more Emersonian than William James in viewing these psychic elements as not only apparently or experientially but genuinely transpersonal, external to some actual extent in that they exist beyond what we usually conceive of as the individual. "The urge to individuation," Jung writes, "gathers together what is scattered and multifarious, and exalts it to the original form of the One, the Primordial Man. In this way our existence as separate beings, our former ego nature, is abolished, the circle of consciousness is widened, and because the paradoxes have been made conscious the sources of conflict are dried up."[13]

It is significant that Jung here uses the ancient and recurring image of the Primordial Man, not to reduce it to a more "basic" psychological explanation, but to elaborate and vitalize his own conceptions, to enrich and put in context his own symbol system. To support the assertion that "Emerson's conception of poetry and the poet belongs to a special Romantic tradition, one larger than American literature and encompassing much of it," R. A. Yoder begins his book on Emerson with the same image: "At the heart of *The American Scholar* is a giant imported myth, so widely assimilated by European muses from 'an unknown antiquity' that any search for an ultimate source is probably beside the point. Emerson's 'old fable' of the 'One Man,' the original whole as distinguished from subsequent fragments, is a version of the traditional 'universal man,' as Kathleen Raine summarizes it, 'the Logos of the Platonists, the Adam Kadmon of the Cabala, the Divine Humanity of Swedenborg and Blake.'"[14] It will be useful, then, to elaborate briefly on the sources and the nature of the Romantic unity-division-reintegration pattern, and discuss some relevant connections with its most recent significant appearance in Jungian psychology.

M. H. Abrams has documented extensively how this pattern derives from, and in turn reshapes, the design of biblical history: "The Biblical scheme . . . begins with the creation of heaven and the earth and ends with the creation of 'a new heaven and a new earth'; the history of man begins with his felicity in an earthly paradise and ends with his felicity in an equivalent paradise. . . . The pattern of Christian history, as Karl Löwith puts it, thus constitutes 'one great detour to reach in the end the beginning.' And in this pattern it is the terminal and not the initial felicity that really matters, for the finish is also the goal, the *telos*, of the entire providential plan."[15] Emerson, for example, often transposed his version of the pattern into biblical terms: "It is very unhappy, but too late to be helped, the discovery we have made that we exist. That discovery is called the Fall of Man" (3:75). And Northrop Frye describes in more detail how this transposition is a general Romantic phenomenon.

> What corresponds to the older myth of an unfallen state, or lost paradise of Eden, is now a sense of an original identity between individual man and nature which has been lost. It may have been something lost in childhood, as in Wordsworth's *Ode on Intimations of Immortality*, or it may be something hazier like a racial collective memory, but it haunts the mind with the same sense of dispossession that the original Eden myth did.
>
> The context of what corresponds to the "fall," or the myth of alienation, changes accordingly. Man has "fallen," not so much into sin as into the original sin of self-consciousness, into his present subject-object relation to nature, where, because his consciousness is what separates him from nature, the primary conscious feeling is one of separation. The alienated man cut off from nature by his consciousness is the Romantic equivalent of post-Edenic Adam.[16]

It is crucial both to this study and to a fuller understanding of Romanticism that "nature" be understood not exclusively as something external to the psyche but as including those aspects of the mind not directly apprehended by consciousness to be part of itself. That is, the ego, in developing and strengthening itself, creates a split within the individual as well as between the individual and the outside world. In the reintegration phase of the pattern, there is a direct relationship between the healing of the two splits, as Emerson suggests: "The problem of restoring to the world original and eternal beauty is solved by the redemption of the soul. . . . The reason why the world lacks unity, and lies broken and in heaps, is because man is disunited with himself" (1:73–74). Our initial experience of being in the world, then, is just that, an experience of totality that becomes divided as soon as we perceive and act on the world in specialized ways. The very opposition of world and self is not an existential given, but the creation of the lapsed consciousness. As Bronson Alcott writes in his journal: "Spirit and Matter, Man and Nature, are the two members of that original undivided synthesis that is the ground and the heart of the Spirit of Man."[17] Or, as Neumann says in more technical language: "We pay a heavy price for the sharpness of our conscious knowledge, which is based on the separation of the psychic systems and which breaks down the one world into the polarity of psyche and world. This price is a drastic curtailment of the reality that we experience."[18]

The very act of creating or apprehending a symbol is, as we have seen, a bridge across the rift, a way of reuniting psyche and world. The centrality and function of creative activity in Jungian psychology is essentially Romantic, a way of recapturing at a higher level of consciousness the original identity Frye describes. As Neumann goes on to say: "The experience of the one reality, which both phylogenetically and ontogenetically precedes the experience of reality by the differentiated consciousness, is eminently 'symbolic.' . . . There is nothing mystical about the symbolical unitary reality, and it is not beyond our experience; it is the world that is always experienced where the polarization of inside and outside, resulting from the separation of the psychic systems, has not yet been effected or is no longer in force."[19]

The parallels in conception and in approach between Romanticism and Jungian thought are underscored and, to some extent, explained by tracing Jung's basic ideas to their roots. Henri Ellenberger, whose book *The Discovery of the Unconscious* is the most detailed history of psychiatry, writes: "Jung's analytic psychology, like Freud's psychoanalysis, is a late offshoot of Romanticism, but psychoanalysis is also the heir of positivism, scientism, and Darwinism, whereas analytical psychology rejects that heritage and returns to the unaltered sources of psychiatric Romanticism and philosophy of nature."[20] Like the German idealistic philosophers, Jung was steeped in Kant's epistemology,[21] and like them he directed much effort toward resolving the dualities of phenomenon and noumenon, mind and world, embedded in that epistemology. Jung's "collective unconscious," or, as he later and more felicitously termed it, "the objective psyche," is at least as much an inheritance from his cultural and intellectual background as an empirical hypothesis. Jung's own main criticism of Freud's psychoanalysis is its "purely rationalistic conception of the unconscious,"[22] an entity that by its very nature cannot be rationalized. Ellenberger's summary of evidence on the relations between Jung and the German Romantics is here quoted at some length, especially because two of the figures mentioned, Schelling and Fichte, bear directly on the reading of Poe's "Morella" in the next chapter:

> According to Leibbrand, Jung's system cannot be conceived without Schelling's philosophy. Rose Mehlich found parallels between Fichte's concepts of the soul and some of Jung's basic assertions. Other parallels can be drawn between Jung's psychology and the philosophy of G. H. von Schubert, and what the latter explained in philosophical terms E. T. A. Hoffmann utilized as a philosophical background for his novel. Like von Schubert, Hoffmann depicted the coexistence in each individual of an individual soul (the ego) and of another psychic principle related to the activity of the World Soul (the self). The individual may at times become conscious of the World Soul; these moments are called "cosmic moments" by von Schubert and "exalted states" (*erhöhte Zustände*) by Hoffmann.[23]

An even more direct link is the physician and philosopher Carl Gustav Carus, who wrote in what for Jung was a crucial book,

Psyche, published in 1846: "The rapport of consciousness with the external cosmos increases when it descends into the unconscious. . . . The unconscious is the *primordial source of life*."[24]

It would be shortsighted, however, to begin with Romanticism itself in examining the backgrounds of Jung's thought. As Jung himself says, "The psychology of the unconscious that began with C. G. Carus took up the trail that had been lost by the alchemists. This happened, remarkably enough, at a moment in history when the aspirations of the alchemists had found their highest poetic expression in Goethe's *Faust*."[25] This quotation supports Ellenberger's statement: "Those Romantic philosophers who were Jung's more direct sources had themselves a long series of predecessors, from the Gnostics and the alchemists to Paracelsus, Boehme, Swedenborg. . . . Some of these men were hailed by Jung as pioneers of the psychology of the unconscious."[26] Jung not only explicitly credited these pioneers, but in very specific and deeply rooted ways assimilated and absorbed much of their thought into his own: his study and analysis of these visionary traditions and figures in turn shaped his own terms and structures. And we need to go back even further and more extensively than Ellenberger suggests. For example, Jung borrowed both the term and the notion of *enantiodromia*, where processes are extended so far they turn into their opposites, from Heraclitus. James Hillman notes that Jung "is the immediate ancestor in a long line that stretches back through Freud, Dilthey, Coleridge, Schelling, Vico, Ficino, Plotinus, and Plato to Heraclitus—with even more branches yet to be traced."[27]

As Hillman suggests, there is nothing as simple here as a straight-line progression, and various scholars would draw up different lists with varying emphases,[28] but there is a broad matrix of thought stretching across the centuries, from which both Romanticism and Jungian psychology arise. To some, this matrix has become a single Occult Tradition, or even more presumptuously "*the* Tradition," or simply "tradition." But only the most extreme of nominalists would deny that the relationships, the influences, the symmetries are there, and that they must be taken into account even if they cannot be fully and clearly delineated. To ignore them can lead to historical and methodological distortions, as when Esther Harding suggests that similar imagery in Revelation, in Blake's work, and in Jung's psychology underscores the universal truth of the last.[29] But as Kathleen Raine points out: "Jung's psychology has its roots in this tradition, and a very great part of Blake's affinity with Jung may be explained without recourse to analytical psychology: Blake and Jung both studied the Neoplatonists, the Gnostics, and the alchemists. In restoring meaning to myth and symbol, Jungian psychology has indeed reopened for my generation a lost world of thought and experience."[30] What Raine seems to take away in the first sentence, she gives back in the second: Jung's work is not just another outcropping or redaction of the "tradition," but a detailed analytic exploration of it. A point that Raine tends to elide, however, is that Blake's work also is a critical examination of the tradition, as well as an intensely symbolic version of it.

For although modern scholars, most notably M. H. Abrams, have reconstructed and reconnected the occulted but traditional backgrounds of Romanticism, the major Romantic writers were sophisticatedly aware of their heritage. Emerson epitomizes this awareness in a single sentence: "Hegel preëxists in Proclus, and, long before, in Heraclitus and Parmenides" (8:180). At a superficial glance, Heraclitus, the philosopher of movement and flux, may seem to be the antithesis of Parmenides, the philosopher of static being, yet the Neoplatonist and the modern dialectician help us see the ways in which each man's thought implies and incorporates that of the other, the ways in which each is his own dialectician. Emerson also writes that "any history of philosophy fortifies my faith, by showing me that what high dogmas I had supposed were the rare and late fruit of cumulative culture, and only now possible to some recent Kant or Fichte,—were the prompt improvisations of the earliest inquirers; of Parmenides, Heraclitus, and Xenophanes" (1:160). Both statements parallel Coleridge's observation in the *Biographia* that the "Dynamic Philosophy" is "no other than the system of Pythagoras and of Plato revived and purified."[31]

But it is still Emerson, the frequent disparager of the past, who is most rhapsodic and detailed about "the tradition":

> I cannot recite, even thus rudely, laws of the intellect, without remembering that lofty and sequestered class who have been its prophets and oracles, the high-priesthood of the pure reason, the *Trismegisti*, the expounders of the principles of thought from age to age. . . . This band of grandees, Hermes, Heraclitus, Empedocles, Plato, Plotinus, Olympiodorus, Proclus, Synesius and the rest, have somewhat so vast in their logic, so primary in their thinking, that it seems antecedent to all the ordinary distinctions of rhetoric and literature, and to be at once poetry and music and dancing and astronomy and mathematics. I am present at the sowing of the seed of the world. [2:345–46]

Although Emerson here is not specific about what these vast and primary laws are, they are no doubt related to the algebra of consciousness we have seen in his essay "Plato." And although this series has an appropriately eclectic ring to it, it is predominantly Neoplatonic. More modern links in the golden chain are added at the beginning of "Plato": "How many great men Nature is incessantly sending up out of night, to be *his* men,—Platonists! the Alexandrians, a constellation of genius; the Elizabethans, not less; Sir Thomas More, Henry More, John Hales, John Smith, Lord Bacon, Jeremy Taylor, Ralph Cudworth, Sydenham, Thomas Taylor; Marcilius Ficinus and Picus Mirandola" (4:40).

Indeed, Neoplatonism stands second only to the design of biblical history in its influence and centrality both for Emerson in particular and for Romanticism in general.[32] As M. H. Abrams writes, "The basic categories of characteristic post-Kantian philosophy, and of the thinking of many philosophical-minded poets, can be viewed as highly elaborated and sophisticated variations upon the Neoplatonic paradigm of a primal unity and goodness, an emanation into multiplicity which is *ipso facto* a lapse into evil and suffering, and a return to unity and goodness."[33] Of the names Emerson mentions, Thomas Taylor is of particular significance. A Neoplatonist by firm personal conviction, he published his monumental five-volume *Works of Plato* in 1804. This work was the most complete English translation at the time, and the one that most shaped the mind of mid-nineteenth-century America.[34] In *English Traits*, Emerson reports a conversation with Wordsworth: "I told him it was not creditable that no one in all the country knew anything of Thomas Taylor, the Platonist, whilst in every American library his translations are found" (5:295). Aside from presenting Plato through a Neoplatonic glass, Taylor made available translations and commentaries on the Orphic Hymns and Neoplatonists of late antiquity, such as Plotinus, Proclus, Iamblichus, Porphyry. This work had the most immediate and important influence on Emerson and Alcott,[35] and through these men and various other directions and indirections the impact on American Romanticism was considerable. When James Hillman writes of the thematic and stylistic similarities between Neoplatonism and archetypal psychology, we find his description at least as appropriate for American Romanticism: "This body of thought . . . is subtle, complex, and ambiguous, a composite of thinking, erotic feeling, and imagination. It is more mythic and exhortative than expositional and discursive; it persuades through rhetoric rather than proving through logic, preferring to be evocative and visionary rather than explanatory. . . . It delighted in surprising juxtapositions and reversals of ideas, for it regarded the soul as ever in movement, without definite positions, a borderline concept between spirit and matter."[36]

Just as it is wrong, however, to isolate Jungian psychology from its cultural contexts and to claim that it provides a universal system under which all others can be subsumed, it would be equally reductive to overextend the argument thus far and view all similarities as a result of direct historical continuities, as only a series of sources and influences. To take just the last topic, we must contend with Emerson's assertion that "I read Proclus, and sometimes Plato, as I might read a dictionary, for a mechanical help to fancy and the imagination. I read for lustres, as if one should use a fine picture in a chromatic experiment, for its rich

colors" (3:233). Although we might be wary of taking this statement at face value—the very light metaphor suggests a deep
immersion in Neoplatonic thought—it is also inaccurate to read
Emerson primarily as a Neoneoplatonist. We would feel more
comfortable applying this label to his friend Bronson Alcott, who
writes in his journal for February 1833: "The observation and
record of results in the experience of my two children, though
extremely crude and unsatisfactory, occupied a place in my attention. The stream of thought which had begun to flow in one direction and to absorb all the other rivulets as contributions to itself,
hastened onward gradually toward the ocean of universality and
infinitude, the primal fountain of inexhaustible energy. . . . The
finite is but the return of the soul on the path of the infinite—the
wheeling orb attracted toward, and yet preserved in the cycle of,
the central sphere."[37] This passage reads like a compendium, in
imagery and idea, of all the texts and traditions we have mentioned so far, but particularly of Neoplatonism. And yet Odell
Shepard, Alcott's biographer and editor of the journals, claims
that it was written before Alcott had read Taylor's Plato and his
other translations and that the ideas may indeed have come
"originally" from Alcott's own observations.[38] Though this claim
does strain credulity, we must at least be open to the possibility
that Alcott's own dispositions and observations led him to read
and study the authors he did, rather than vice versa.

Fortunately, for the purposes of this book, there is no need to
reach definitive conclusions on this complex issue. As a middle
position, though, we can suggest that the unity-division-reintegration pattern forms what David Brent has called a "cognitive
archetype."[39] That is, given the nature of the human psyche and
the basic conditions of human existence, such a pattern is likely to
emerge, although in ways significantly different in various cultures and in various stages of a culture. As Mircea Eliade writes:

Man feels himself torn and separate. He often finds it difficult properly to explain to himself the nature of this separation, for sometimes he feels himself to be cut off from
"something" *powerful*, "something" utterly *other* than

himself. . . . Ultimately, it is the wish to recover this lost
unity that has caused man to think of the opposites as complementary aspects of a single reality. It is as a result of
such existential experiences caused by the need to transcend
the opposites, that the first theological and philosophical
speculations were elaborated. Before they became the main
philosophical concepts, the One, the Unity, the Totality
were desires revealed in myths and beliefs and expressed
in rites and mystical techniques.[40]

The crucial point here is that American Romanticism represents yet a later stage in the process, where the One, the Unity,
the Totality are divested of much of their philosophical and theological status and reattached to the original conditions, feelings,
aspirations from which they were abstracted. We have already
seen, for example, Poe's stress on intuition, on knowledge welling
up from the mind itself, as the basis for apparently metaphysical
statements about the One. This emphasis increases dramatically
as *Eureka* moves towards its conclusion: "The *phaenomena* on
which our conclusions must at this point depend, are merely spiritual shadows, but not the less thoroughly substantial" (16:311).
The final vision of the book is introduced with the following sentences: "I have spoken of *Memories* that haunt us during our
youth. They sometimes pursue us even in our Manhood:—assume
gradually less and less indefinite shapes:—now and then speak to
us with low voices" (16:313). Poe's stance towards metaphysical
ideas often anticipates Jung's phenomenological approach. Jung
says that "the universal belief in spirits is a direct expression of
the complex structure of the unconscious,"[41] and that "the idea
of God is an absolutely necessary psychological function of an
irrational nature, which has nothing whatever to do with the
question of God's existence."[42] Poe says: "That the belief in ghosts,
or in a Deity, or in a future state, or in anything else credible
or incredible—that any such belief is universal, demonstrates
nothing more than . . . the identity of construction in the human
brain" (16:115).

For Emerson, metaphysics in itself would seem to be a more central and explicit concern, and it would be misleading to deny this component in his work. But as we follow the movement of his own development, we see an increasing interest in the roots and psychological implications of metaphysics that reflects in microcosm the general movement we are tracing. Emerson himself says: "As religious philosophy advances, men will cease to say 'the future state' & will say instead 'the whole being.'"[43] He defends Plato from the charge that the philosopher did not develop a satisfactory theory of the universe by maintaining that the endeavor itself is futile and misguided: "No power of genius has ever yet had the smallest success in explaining existence. The perfect enigma remains" (4:78). Emerson's late essay "Natural History of Intellect" begins with an attack on metaphysics detached from our minute-by-minute consciousness of living in the world: "'Tis the gnat grasping the world. All these exhaustive theories appear indeed a false and vain attempt to . . . analyze the Primal Thought" (12:11). As opposed to system and abstraction, Emerson's own method will be to "write anecdotes of the intellect; a sort of Farmer's Almanac of mental moods. I confine my ambition to true reporting of its play in natural action" (12:10–11). One of the primary facts he encounters and describes as best he can is "that unknown country in which all the rivers of our knowledge have their fountains, and which, by its qualities and structure, determines both the nature of the waters and the direction in which they flow" (12:30). This is not to argue, however, that Emerson reaches a pure or simple position of subjectivity, because this concept implies a distinction neither he nor Jung is willing to accept. As Emerson says of the ideal transcendentalist: "His experience inclines him to behold the procession of facts you call the world, as flowing perpetually outward from an invisible, unsounded centre in himself, centre alike of him and of them, and necessitating him to regard all things as having a subjective or relative existence, relative to that aforesaid Unknown Centre of him" (1:334).

More direct are Whitman's words that "there is no object so soft but it makes a hub for the wheel'd universe" (86). Every object that the mind encounters is to its own self a subject, and the more the mind can apprehend this, the more it can transcend its own subjectivity. Whitman's stress on the immediate felt experience is an attempt not to narrow the field of poetry, but to widen it meaningfully. In "Song of Myself" he asks the reader to consider "the origin of all poems" (30): "The saints and sages in history— but you yourself? / Sermons, creeds, theology—but the fathomless human brain . . ." (78). Whitman wants to speak from a position of what Neumann would call the symbolical unitary reality, as is suggested by a short poem strategically placed in the "Inscriptions" section: "Beginning my studies, the first step pleas'd me so much, / The mere fact consciousness, . . . / I have hardly gone and hardly wish'd to go any farther, / But stop and loiter all the time to sing it in ecstatic songs" (9). Concepts and creeds are only indirect ways of speaking about the more basic and central fact: "The myth of heaven indicates the soul" (432).

Of all American Romantics, however, the one who most consistently held this focus both as theme and as angle of vision is Emily Dickinson.

> The Brain—is wider than the Sky—
> For—put them side by side—
> The one the other will contain
> With ease—and You—beside. . . .
>
> The Brain is just the weight of God—
> For—Heft them—Pound for Pound—
> And they will differ—if they do—
> As Syllable from Sound—   [632]

An important point about these lines is that consciousness is viewed as containing the "You," the sense of individual identity, instead of being limited to it. Also, if there is a difference between syllable and sound, it is that between articulated human meaning and sheer being.[44] Elsewhere, Dickinson writes: "Captivity is Consciousness— / So's Liberty" (384). Behind both the ecstasy in the knowledge that "The Soul's Superior instants / Occur to Her—alone—"(306) and the anguish and isolation of "The Soul condemned to be— / Attended by a single Hound / It's own identity" (822), is a sense of the radical immediacy and irreducibility of experience. Whereas with Poe, Emerson, and Whitman there is an important tendency to move cosmology and metaphysics constantly into psychology and phenomenology, with Dickinson we see this movement virtually completed. The movement itself, however, does not clarify or simplify existence, but rather intensifies it, as Dickinson suggests: "Paradise is no Journey because it is within—but for that very cause though—it is the most Arduous of Journeys."[45] Emerson, particularly in the Divinity School Address, stresses that Christ's incarnation is to be understood symbolically, as a possibility open to everyone: "One man was true to what is in you and me" (1:128). But Dickinson sees also that the same is true of the crucifixion, and that "Gethsemane— / Is but a Province—in the Being's Centre—" (553). The variant reading for the last two words is "Human Centre."

The ways in which metaphysical elements, especially the paradigm set forth here, are internalized and used to understand and depict psychological dynamics in Poe, Emerson, Whitman, and Dickinson will be examined specifically in the next four chapters. We can conclude this chapter by seeing the process in microcosm in passages from Hawthorne and Melville. The following is a complete entry from Hawthorne's journals:

> The human Heart to be allegorized as a cavern; at the entrance there is sunshine and flowers growing about it. You step within, but a short distance, and begin to find yourself surrounded with a terrible gloom, and monsters of divers kinds; it seems like Hell itself. You are bewildered, and wander long without hope. At last a light strikes upon you. You press towards it yon, and find yourself in a region that seems, in some sort, to reproduce the flowers and sunny beauty of the entrance, but all perfect. These are the depths of the heart, or of human nature, bright and peaceful; the gloom and terror lie deep; but deeper still is this eternal beauty.[46]

The primarily spatial metaphor is given a temporal emphasis as well, by being set forth in narrative terms. The use of the second person increases both the immediacy and the universality of the experience, however allegorized and stylized. The experience suggests both the progression of the psyche over a lifetime and certain intense periods within it, dark nights of the soul followed by radiant dawns. The religious and metaphysical imagery—"Hell," "eternal beauty"—is used explicitly for symbols involving the "human Heart." In looking forward to Jung, Hawthorne looks back toward Bunyan and Spenser, but even further back toward Plato's allegory of the cave in book seven of *The Republic*. In Plato's allegory, however, the locus of ultimacy is eventually discovered by leaving the cave and looking up at the sun. In contrast to this ascending movement, Hawthorne's imagery supports Northrop Frye's contention about a crucial shift in vision: "The metaphorical structure of Romantic poetry tends to move inside and downward instead of outside and upward, hence the creative world is deep within, and so is heaven or the place of the presence of God."[47]

There is similar movement and structure in "The Grand Armada" chapter of *Moby-Dick*. A whale struck by Queequeg's harpoon draws the boat Ishmael is in into the chaotic midst of the entire herd: "As the swift monster drags you deeper and deeper into the frantic shoal, you bid adieu to circumspect life and only exist in a delirious throb."[48] Although the whalers themselves have initiated the process, they are now at the mercy of larger, stronger powers, which finally glide the boat into a sleek, an "enchanted calm which they say lurks at the heart of every commotion."[49] This surface calm is only a window on a deeper, more wondrous calm beneath: "Some of the subtlest secrets of the seas seemed divulged to us in this enchanted pond. We saw young Leviathan amours in the deep."[50] Ishmael's psychologizing mind draws a linked analogy to his own experience: "And thus, though surrounded by circle upon circle of consternations and affrights, did these inscrutable creatures at the centre freely and fearlessly indulge in all peaceful concernments; yea, serenely revelled in dalliance and delight. But even so, amid the tornadoed Atlantic of my being, do I myself still for ever centrally disport in mute calm; and while ponderous planets of unwaning woe revolve round me, deep down and deep inland there I still bathe me in eternal mildness of joy."[51]

This is not to say, however, that these passages give us the informing vision behind the works of Hawthorne and Melville. It is significant that Hawthorne never wrote the piece he had sketched out. And although one critic has isolated from the children's books Hawthorne's ideal myth as the quest encounter with monsters who haunt dark caves, resulting in a return with enhanced powers,[52] in most of the tales and longer romances, the deeper we proceed into the cavern, the more formidable and inexorable becomes the heart of darkness. Further, any image Melville gives of the psyche can be countered or undercut by another image in *Moby-Dick*. And yet both these passages help explain significant counter-tendencies within the generally tragic thrusts of the works. Pearl, a wild, agitated child restlessly and unconsciously trying to bring out the truth, is transformed and made whole by Dimmesdale's confession: "A spell was broken . . . she would grow up amid human joy and sorrow, nor for ever do battle with the world, but be a woman in it."[53] A similar magic saves Ishmael when the Pequod and the rest of the crew are destroyed by Moby-Dick: "Round and round, then . . . I did revolve. Till, gaining that vital centre, the black bubble upward burst; and now, liberated by reason of its cunning spring, and owing to its great buoyancy, rising with great force, the coffin life-buoy shot lengthwise from the sea, fell over, and floated by my side."[54] Possible reasons for Ishmael's survival have been put forth by critics as the power of genuine friendship, the redemptive force of language, the lack of metaphysical dogmatism. But subsuming all of these is the meeting and mixing of opposites in the symbol of the coffin life-buoy. As Melville writes in a poem:

Instinct and study; love and hate;
Audacity—reverence. These must mate,
And fuse with Jacob's mystic heart,
To wrestle with the angel—Art.[55]

IV.

ANIMATOPOEIA:

SIRENS OF THE SELF

This meeting and fusing of contrarieties, the *coincidentia oppositorum*, is most often and most effectively symbolized by the related imagery of marriage and sexual union. We have noted Emerson's use of Asia as an image of the unknown but intuited aspects of the psyche, but we can further observe that he referred to his wife Lydian as "mine Asia." Also, we see in the journal entry quoted in Chapter 2 the phrase "marry mind to nature," which echoes Wordsworth's lines about the paradises within:

> For the discerning intellect of Man,
> When wedded to this goodly universe
> In love and holy passion, shall find these
> A simple produce of the common day.
> —I, long before the blissful hour arrives,
> Would chaunt, in lonely peace, the spousal verse
> Of this great consummation. . . .[1]

Behind these Romantic utterances, though, lies a traditional imagery that has its roots in the Bible, especially the Book of Revelation, which recapitulates and condenses the many scattered references to the sacred marriage between God and his chosen people, Christ and the Heavenly City, the Lamb and his bride. This imagery takes on increasing importance in the occulted traditions mentioned in the last chapter.[2] In Hermetical alchemy, for example, the spiritual goal of union is signified by the *hieros gamos*, the sacred marriage of the King and the Queen, Sol and Luna, sulphur and mercury. Out of these images and thought patterns evolved a tenet of Romantic psychology, reaching its most extensive formulation in Jungian thought, that each person is psychologically androgynous, and that the contrasexual element represents the unknown, unrealized part that has to be integrated with consciousness. A. J. L. Busst has traced in detail the development of this idea primarily in French Romanticism, pointing out figures such as Pierre Leroux, who reinterprets in psychological terms the occult belief that Adam was originally androgynous: "Like Adam, rehabilitated man will be androgynous only psychologically, in that in him subject and object, self and non-self will be united. . . . it is the doctrine of the *retour à l'unité par la connaisance*."[3] In American Romanticism, Margaret Fuller formulates this theory most explicitly: "Male and female represent the two sides of the great radical dualism. But, in fact, they are perpetually passing into one another. Fluid hardens to solid, solid rushes to fluid. There is no wholly masculine man, no purely feminine woman."[4]

We can see these ideas as immediate psychic realities in the works of Edgar Allan Poe and Emily Dickinson, where a figure of the opposite sex, surrounded by an aura of the mysterious and numinous, holds out the promise of harmonious unity, of initiation into the higher secrets, a promise usually accompanied, though, by the possibilities of dissolution and death. This chapter, which explores Poe's vision of the psychological feminine, will be complemented by an examination of the psychological masculine in Dickinson in Chapter 7. This examination does not align itself closely with the corresponding Logos (rational and masculine)/Eros (intuitive and feminine) distinction that is overstressed in Jungian psychology.[5] Instead, with both authors the contrasexual is treated primarily as the non-ego, according to the contours of a particular text or set of texts. Also, in our investigation, we have to make distinctions within larger categories such as "intellect"; several of Poe's women characters, for example, have greater and broader intellects than their partners, as well as access to other ways of experiencing, from which their partners ultimately turn. To merely superimpose the Logos/Eros distinction on the masculine/feminine opposition in these stories would not be productive. Similarly, a Jungian concept like the "anima" helps because it has been clearly and sensitively developed, whereas the corresponding concept of "animus" is of little use to us in analyzing Dickinson's male figures.

In this chapter, then, we examine some of Poe's work that can be read as what Maurice Barrès calls "a history of the soul with its two elements, feminine and male."[6] Most of Poe's female figures should strictly not even be called "projections," because the word implies that there is enough of an external person to serve as a reflecting screen. Poe's creations usually exist purely on the plane of what he would call "ideality" and therefore are less distorting to our view of real women than those of other authors who hopelessly confound their own dreams and fears with the inhabitants of this middle earth.

At this point, it may be helpful to put before us a distinction implicit in Jung's work and set forth in detail in Neumann's analysis of the feminine in man's psyche, that between the "elementary" and the "transformative" character.[7] The former is associated with the initial unconscious state from which the ego detaches itself, but which in its early stages still feels as an encompassing presence, as the realm of "The Mothers."[8] The "transformative" character, on the other hand, points toward future development, toward a widening of the ego and an integration with the rest of the self. It is this aspect of the feminine vectored toward individuation that properly should be called the "anima." This distinction frees us from identifying every feminine image with fixation at a more infantile state, and recognizes there are psychic forces moving us into the future as well as ones created by the past.

One of Poe's best lyrics can serve as a classic description of the anima in its unambiguously positive aspect. "To Helen" has been widely discussed, but its nature as a poem of individuation and its background in illuminist traditions have not been fully understood.

Helen, thy beauty is to me
　　Like those Nicéan barks of yore,
That gently, o'er a perfumed sea,
　　The weary, way-worn wanderer bore
　　To his own native shore.

On desperate seas long wont to roam,
　　Thy hyacinth hair, thy classic face,
Thy Naiad airs have brought me home
　　To the glory that was Greece,
　　And the grandeur that was Rome.

Lo! in yon brilliant window-niche
　　How statue-like I see thee stand,
　　The agate lamp within thy hand!
Ah, Psyche, from the regions which
　　Are Holy-Land![9]

Poe's address of Helen as "Psyche" restores Apuleius's original use of the name as at once a mortal transformed into a goddess and as the soul itself. Just as Keats in his "Ode to Psyche" had transferred the external figure into the sphere of his own mind— "Yes, I will be thy priest and build a fane / In some untrodden region of my mind"—Poe's poem is about the expansion of consciousness and the harmonizing of the soul. The reason this takes the form of an encounter with the feminine is suggested by Jung's comment that for a man "what is not-I, not masculine, is most probably feminine."[10] This explanation accords with Simone de Beauvoir's notion of man's fundamental experience of woman as the Other: "Man feminizes the ideal he sets up before him as the essential Other, because woman is the material representation of alterity; that is why almost all allegories, in language as in pictorial representation are women. Woman is Soul and Idea, but she is also a mediatrix between them. . . . In all doctrines that unify Nature and Spirit she appears as Harmony, Reason, Truth."[11]

To be even more specific, Helen is not only part of the speaker's own self, but the focal symbol in which consciousness and the unconscious join. As suggested already, the primary means of individuation is the symbol and the progression of the poem illuminates this process. In the first stanza, Helen's beauty is compared to a ship bearing an unnamed but suggestively mythological wanderer back to the land of his birth. In the second stanza, the speaker links himself to this wanderer, who was at first only part of an extended simile. Thus, the reverie that Helen has inspired has already moved the speaker closer to "home"—a word that stands as the central rhyme of the poem—by weaving him into the fabric of the mythopoeic realm he is evoking. The Helen of the third stanza is even more deeply embedded in this realm, posed and "statue-like," addressed as the last goddess of classical mythology.

To recapture some of the original resonances of this imagery, we can juxtapose it with a passage from Thomas Taylor, the English Neoplatonist introduced in the last chapter. In an introduction to his own translation of Plotinus's *Concerning the Beautiful*, Taylor explains that his work is addressed to that person

> who considers himself in the language of Empedocles, as
> *Heaven's exile, straying from the orb of light;*
> and who so ardently longs for a return to his true country,
> that to him, as to Ulysses, when fighting for Ithaca,
> *Slow seems the sun to move, the hours to roll;*
> *His native home deep-imag'd in his soul.*[12]

Taylor, following Neoplatonic tradition, continues to allegorize and interiorize the myth of Ulysses as the story of the soul finding and recognizing its true nature, its original unity with the One. He points out that Ulysses did not recognize Ithaca as his own homeland until the goddess of wisdom purged his vision.

> *Now lift thy longing eyes, while I restore,*
> *The pleasing prospect of thy native shore....*

Let us then humbly supplicate the irradiations of wisdom, and follow Plotinus as our divine guide to the beatific vision of the Beautiful itself: for, in this alone we can find perfect repose, and repair those destructive clefts and chinks of the soul which its departure from the light of good . . . have introduced.[13]

Poe's poem is also about the return to the original unity of the soul, to "home," to the entire "Psyche," as Helen is finally called. In the Neoplatonic tradition, "Psyche" is the *anima mundi*, the world soul, corresponding to what Poe at the end of *Eureka* calls the "general consciousness." By portraying her holding a lamp, Poe emphasizes her similarity to the mythological Psyche, who, against Eros's injunction, lifted a candle to behold her immortal lover. Neumann, who has analyzed this story in detail, sees this act as crucial: "Once she sees Eros in the light, Psyche sets the love principle of encounter and individuation beside the principle of fascinating attraction and the fertility of the species."[14] Further, the name "Helen" itself means "bearer of light"—light, the universal symbol of consciousness. The original state of unity, implied by words such as "native shore" and "home," has been recovered but at a more complex, self-reflexive level of awareness. Opposites like male/female, conscious/unconscious, self/other are not collapsed into each other but harmoniously integrated.

Other critics, most notably Richard Wilbur,[15] have noted imagistic connections between Helen and other Poe women, but have not elaborated on the significances of these similarities. Perhaps the most obvious physical convergences are with the Marchesa Aphrodite of "The Assignation." As we first glimpse her, she too is depicted as standing "statue-like" in an entranceway, her "classical head" surrounded by "curls like those of the young hyacinth" (2:111), just as Ligeia, too, has "hyacinthine" tresses (2:250). The Marchesa is the inspiration of a lyric almost as melodic and evocative as "To Helen."

Thou wast that all to me, love,
  For which my soul did pine—
A green isle in the sea, love,
  A fountain and a shrine,
All wreathed with fairy fruits and flowers;
  And all the flowers were mine.

The next stanza, though, suggests the melancholy and despair
that such a vision can bring, as well as foreshadowing the union-
in-death of the tale's end.

Ah, dream too bright to last;
  Ah, starry Hope that didst arise
But to be overcast!
  A voice from out the Future cries
"Onward!"—but o'er the Past
  (Dim gulf!) my spirit hovering lies,
Mute, motionless, aghast!   [2:120]

The purported author of these lines is the Byronesque hero of
the tale, called simply "the stranger" by the narrator and "the
visionary" in the original title. And the story is not as much a
sketch or satire of any specific Romantic figure as it is a diagnosis
of some of the dangers involved in the entire Romantic endeavor.
As with "The Haunted Palace" in "The Fall of the House of Usher,"
Poe composed and published the poem first under his own name,
so that both stories can be read as courageous and subtle self-
analyses of the aspirations and nature of Poe's own poetic sensi-
bility. It is clear from the very first sentence that the attraction of
the Marchesa Aphrodite has its origins in the visionary's own
psyche: "Ill-fated and mysterious man!—bewildered in the brilliancy of thine own imagination, and fallen in the flames of thine
own youth!" (2:109). The first paragraph ends with the seemingly
rhetorical question: "Who blame thee for thy visionary hours, or
denounce those occupations as a wasting away of life, which were
but the overflowings of thine everlasting energies?" (2:109–10).
One thinks of Barrès again, who writes in a letter: "Amidst soli-

tude and my sobbings, I have sometimes discovered more real voluptuousness than in the arms of a woman."[16] And elsewhere: "It is I alone whom I love for the feminine perfume of my soul."[17]

In the opening scene, the visionary plunges headlong into a Venetian canal at midnight, into "the secrets of her silent waters," to retrieve "the treasure which was to be found, alas! only within the abyss" (2:109, 111). The treasure is the child of the Marchesa Aphrodite, whom she has—perhaps intentionally—let slip from her arms. The visionary's success in this venture parallels the episode of the night-sea journey undertaken by heroes in legends and myths: the motif suggests a victory of the ego strong enough to descend to the depths of the unconscious, and reemerge intact and strengthened, with a widening of knowledge and power, a spiritual rebirth. These symbolic resonances underlie the Marchesa's oracular response to the rescue: " 'Thou hast conquered—' " (2:115). The visionary's victory, though, is pyrrhic and temporary, for the Marchesa immediately sets forth a task even more dangerous, luring the hero toward an even deeper abyss, the "hollow vale" of death, as it is called both in the epigram to the tale and in the words quoted at the end by the visionary. In the only other words she speaks in the tale, the Marchesa says: "Thou has conquered—one hour after sunrise—we shall meet—so let it be!" (2:114).

If we bear in mind the lines of the poem—"o'er the Past / (Dim gulf!) my spirit hovering lies / Mute, motionless, aghast!"—we can see that the visionary's death can be viewed as the equivalent of psychic dissolution, and the tale in a wider sense as the portrayal of what Neumann calls "uroboric incest." The adjective "uroboric" comes from the ancient Greek figure of the primal dragon or snake, self-begetting, biting its own tail, and the image figures prominently in Renaissance and Romantic thought.[18] Neumann uses it to stand for the range of analogous symbols in other cultures and mythologies that suggest the primordial unconscious from which the ego arises. He also stresses that "incest" be "understood symbolically, not concretistically and sexually."[19] He sees "uroboric incest," then, as regressive and ultimately ego-destroying: "Many forms of nostalgia and longing signify no more than a return to uroboric incest and self-dissolution, from the *unio mystica* of the saint to the drunkard's craving for unconsciousness and the 'death-romanticism' of the Germanic races."[20]

The Marchesa is indeed an anima figure, but her ultimate effect is to lead the ego too far beyond itself, to a transcendence that is inextricable from destruction. We recall that in the original myth, Aphrodite is the enemy and harasser of Psyche and would rather keep Eros in an incestuous filial relationship than have him marry Psyche as an equal. But the two are really different aspects of the same psychic complex that can lead either to the dissolution just described or to a creative reintegration. The difference between the two is enormous, but they are separated by only a hairsbreadth. The crucial factor is the strength and stance of the ego itself, so it is appropriate that the bulk of "The Assignation" focuses on the character and surroundings of the visonary himself. " 'To dream has been the business of my life. I have therefore framed for myself, as you see, a bower of dreams' " (2:123). The bower here mentioned is a room furnished with disparate art objects deliberately juxtaposed to shatter the limitations of time and place in a quest for an absolute magnificence. Further, it is a bower within a bower, as Venice is described as "that city of dim visions . . . a star-beloved Elysium of the sea" (2:109). Put more prosaically and more analytically, the ego seems to be seeking beyond itself too frenetically, prematurely, and absolutely. It rushes in where other Poe narrators—to their downfall as well—fear to tread. The attention lavished on the details— the character, the taste, the poetry of the visionary—suggests that Poe is not merely contributing one more version of the marriage-in-death theme, but further providing an analysis of what is called in the tale "the Genius of Romance" (2:110), the quest for ecstasy in its etymological sense, a standing outside oneself—or, in our terms, one's ego—that may become perilously permanent.

The feminine as it appears in Poe, then, or in any other writer who treats women as psychic externalizations, can be viewed first as either elementary or transformative in character, the Great Mother or the anima. Further, each of these two characters has both a positive and a negative aspect. These categories, however, should be considered not static compartments, but poles in a very complex set of dynamics. "The Assignation," for example, suggests how close in ultimate effect may be the negative anima to the negative aspect of the elementary feminine, the Terrible Mother. The relationships between the negative and positive aspects of the anima itself have a particular relevance to Poe's art and underlie the dramatic tensions in many of the best tales. The narrator of "Morella" describes the sudden reversals of feelings he experiences with his wife: "And then, hour after hour, would I linger by her side, and dwell upon the music of her voice—until, at length, its melody was tainted with terror—and there fell a shadow upon my soul—and I grew pale, and shuddered inwardly at those too unearthly tones. And thus, joy suddenly faded into horror, and the most beautiful became the most hideous, as Hinnon became Ge-Hanna" (2:28). Similarly, the expansion of Ligeia's eyes "at once so delighted and appalled" her husband (2:253). And the narrator of "Berenice," who both loves and fearfully hates the title character, says in what might serve as an epigram for all three stories, "The agonies which *are* have their origin in the ecstasies which *might have been*" (2:16). Neumann writes: "The ambivalent female mana figure may guide the male or beguile him. Side by side with sublimation stands abasement. . . . And how close ecstasy is to madness, enthusiasm to death, creativeness to psychosis, is shown by mythology, by the history of religions, and by the lives of innumerable great men for whom the gift from the depths has spelled doom."[21]

To see more specifically how these dynamics operate, we will examine in detail "Morella," a relatively early story that is particularly suitable for present purposes because of philosophical allusions within the text. The title character's vague, apocryphal appearance emphasizes her ultimate origin in the narrator's own psyche. The syntax of the second sentence—"Thrown by accident into her society many years ago, my soul, from our first meeting, burned with fires it had never before known" (2:27)—encourages the notion that it is specifically the narrator's "soul" to which Morella presents herself, just as the visionary is dazzled by the brilliancy "of his own imagination" (2:109). The narrator tells us that they met by accident and were fated to marry; as we have seen, psychic events that originate beyond the ego are often perceived as coming from the outside, as happening by accident or by fate. Indeed, the more ego-consciousness is developed at the expense of other areas of the psyche, the more likely one is to encounter apparently autonomous forms thrown up from the unconscious as compensatory mechanisms. The rigidity and lopsided development of the narrator's psyche are suggested in the first paragraph by his reaction to the feelings Morella arouses in him: "Bitter and tormenting to my spirit was the gradual conviction that I could in no manner define their unusual meaning, or regulate their vague intensity" (2:27).

His reactions to feelings that are beyond his conscious understanding and control help to explain his ambivalence toward Morella and the one-way nature of their relationship. Morella reaches out to him with love, as the anima seeking recognition and union. The narrator also desires this union to some extent, but for one so out of touch with his unconscious, a venture beyond the ego is fraught with the dangers of psychic upheaval and the overwhelming of the conscious personality. The ecstasy that Morella proffers is, as we have seen, often the obverse side of terror. This Janus face that Morella presents to the narrator is suggested in her very name. Although T. O. Mabbott has found a historical Morella from whom it is likely Poe took the name,[22] the reasons for this choice probably lie in the juxtaposition of a root signifying "death" with another, found in names of other Poe women such as Helen, Lenore, Eleonora, associated with "light."[23]

This ambivalence and confusion emerge in the way the narrator responds to Morella's philosophical studies, which he later calls her "wild tales and thrilling theories" (2:32)—"thrilling" in the sense both of exciting and of terrifying. At first he feels that he can engage in these studies without serious consequences; he is a level-headed, commonsensical person who will not fall prey to any perils of mysticism. Indeed, he protests his positivism almost as much as the narrator of "Ms. Found in a Bottle": "Beyond all things, the study of the German moralists gave me great delight; not from any ill-advised admiration of their eloquent madness, but from the ease with which my habits of rigid thought enabled me to detect their falsities" (2:1). The narrator of "Morella," however, is uneasy enough with this stance to qualify it with three conditional clauses in the space of two sentences: "In all this, if I err not, my reason had little to do. My convictions, or I forget myself, were in no manner acted upon by the ideal, nor was any tincture of the mysticism which I read, to be discovered, unless I am greatly mistaken, either in my deeds or in my thoughts" (2:28). Other references to Morella's studies reveal an important divergence, already pointed out by Eric Carlson in his brief note to the tale: "The citing of Fichte, Schelling, and Locke provide major clues to the opposed views of identity or selfhood represented by Morella and the narrator."²⁴ The narrator's elliptical summary of their studies suggests that either he refuses to accept all of Morella's teachings or that he misunderstands them in a psychologically revealing way.

It is unnecessary to state the exact character of those disquisitions which, growing out of the volumes I have mentioned, formed, for so long a time, almost the sole conversation of Morella and myself. By the learned in what might be termed theological morality they will be readily conceived, and by the unlearned they would, at all events, be little understood. The wild Pantheism of Fichte; the modified Παλιγγενεσια of the Pythagoreans; and, above all, the doctrines of *Identity* as urged by Schelling, were generally the points of discussion presenting the most of beauty to the imaginative Morella. That identity which is termed personal, Mr. Locke, I think, truly defines to consist in the sameness of a rational being. And since by person we understand an intelligent essence having reason, and since there is a consciousness which always accompanies thinking, it is this which makes us all to be that which we call *ourselves*—thereby distinguishing us from other beings that think, and giving us our personal identity. But the *principium individuationis*—the notion of that identity *which at death is or is not lost forever*, was to me—at all times, a consideration of intense interest; not more from the perplexing and exciting nature of its consequences, than from the marked and agitated manner in which Morella mentioned them. [2:28–29]²⁵

Morella's interest in Fichte, Schelling, and the Pythagoreans affirms her belief in a larger unity beyond what we think of as our personal identities. As does *Eureka*, these doctrines view the relationship between this personal identity and an identity with the One as complementary and inverse. Fichte says: "The demand that the I shall become absolute is not a demand for the independence of the I considered as an individual. Individuality implies limitation. The individual I becomes absolute only so far as individuality is laid aside."²⁶ Similarly, the primary meaning of "Identity" in Schelling's writings is the absolute unity of all opposites, as opposed to the "self-identity" of immediate, personal consciousness. Poe's awareness of Schelling's concern with an identity beyond the ego is demonstrated in an early version of "Loss of Breath": "A rapid change was now taking place in my sensations. The last shadows of connection flitted away from my meditations. A storm—a tempest of ideas, vast, novel, and soul-stirring, bore my spirit like a feather afar off. . . . In a very short time Schelling himself would have been satisfied with my entire loss of self-identity" (2:360).

Although Morella is primarily interested in this transcendental view of "identity," the *principium individuationis*, the personal identity, is "at all times, a consideration of intense interest" to the narrator. He discusses this concept in terms of Locke's atomistic, rationalistic philosophy, with phrases associated with the ego's mode of knowing—"the sameness of a rational being," "intelligent essence having reason," "a consciousness which always accompanies thinking." Morella's sense of a transpersonal identity emerges only in the garbled form of speculations on reincarnation, but even here the narrator seems mainly concerned with the continuance after death of the ego-consciousness to which he is so attached. There is no basis for reincarnation in the philosophies of Fichte, Schelling, or Locke, and the narrator's focus on Παλιγγενεσια, the Pythagorean doctrine of the transmigration of souls after death, reveals the selectivity with which he approaches Morella's teachings. For integral to this doctrine is the hope of eventual release from the cycle of death and rebirth, and a reabsorption in the One, an aspect of Pythagoreanism appropriately stressed by Thomas Taylor. This rejoining with the original unity is systematically omitted in the narrator's exposition, but lies, as the missing piece of the puzzle, in the epigraph of the tale: "Itself, by itself solely, *one* everlastingly, and single" (2:27). The "marked and and agitated manner" in which Morella speaks of the *principium individuationis* and its possible existence after death may stem from her exasperation in trying to convince the narrator that there are more things in heaven and earth than are dreamt of in Locke's philosophy.

The vision Morella offers, of a realm of being beyond the confines of the ego, induces in the narrator a sort of spiritual vertigo: "I met the glance of her meaning eyes, and then my soul sickened and became giddy with the giddiness of one who gazes downward into some dreary and unfathomable abyss" (2:29–30). Even the impulsive and courageous visionary stood "pausing a moment upon the verge of the giddy descent" (2:112) before plunging headlong into the waters. The approach-avoidance conflict ultimately becomes unbearable; the narrator turns from Morella completely and wishes for her death. Morella understands the wellsprings of these actions better than her husband, who insulates himself from his own emotions: "She seemed, also, conscious of a cause, to me unknown, for the gradual alienation of my regard" (2:29). She can, moreover, predict the disastrous consequences of the narrator's failure of strength and trust: "'For the hours of thy happiness are over . . . thou shalt bear about thee thy shroud on the earth, as do the Moslemin at Mecca'" (2:31).

Morella as an anima figure cannot be destroyed, only repressed, and this repression will cause a greater disruption in the psyche than any direct confrontation with the unconscious. A symbol released from the unconscious can either be understood and assimilated by the ego or it can be pushed away unfathomed. In the latter case, the symbol can take on qualities of an autonomous splinter psyche, confronting the ego as a hostile foreign body. The birth of Morella's daughter, who draws her first breath the instant her mother draws her last, signifies this irrevocable splitting-off. Any possibilities for a willing union of equals as epitomized in the marriage relationship have been foreclosed. The first Morella, for example, on her own initiative shuns society and attends only to her husband; the second Morella is deliberately isolated from the outside world by the actions of her father. Although fate bound the narrator at the altar to Morella, an even more inexorable and ominous destiny compels the narrator to adore her daughter. The child's rapid, unnatural growth into the resemblance of the mother suggests the hydra-headed nature of repression: "For that her smile was like her mother's I could bear; but then I shuddered at its too perfect *identity*—that her eyes were like Morella's I could endure; but then they too often looked down into the depths of my soul with Morella's own intense and bewildering meaning" (2:32). Thus, Morella's lesson of identity returns with a vengeance. What the narrator saw earlier in the "meaning eyes" of the mother, so like an "unfathomable abyss," he now encounters in the eyes of the daughter—the same "intense and bewildering meaning." Both pairs of eyes bespeak an identity not only with each other, but between themselves and "the depths of [the narrator's] soul." Both contain the lost promise of an identity between the individual and the universe, and between the ego and the self.

As the tale moves towards its conclusion, its basic dynamic becomes clear: the more the narrator tries to stay within the existing limits of his own ego, the more the ego structure crumbles under the strain of holding on to its regressive position. As Jung writes: "When a part of the psyche is split off from consciousness it is only *apparently* inactivated; in actual fact it brings about a possession of the personality, with the result that the individual's aims are falsified in the interests of the split-off part."[27] The narrator becomes less an acting subject and increasingly the object of impulses he perceives as coming from the outside. This condition is reflected in the very syntax of his utterances: "Suspicions, of a nature fearful and exciting, crept in upon my spirit"; "the ceremony of baptism presented to my mind . . . a present deliverance from the terrors of my destiny" (2:32–33). At the baptismal font, where he must finally give a name to his daughter, his "possession" becomes complete; he sees all his actions as instigated by unknown, hostile forces: "What prompted me, then, to disturb the memory of the buried dead? What demon urged me to breathe that sound, which, in its very recollection was wont to make ebb the purple blood in torrents from the temples to the heart? What fiend spoke from the recesses of my soul, when, amid those dim aisles, and in the silence of the night, I whispered within the ears of the holy man the syllables—Morella?" (2:33). With this last word, the narrator not only names his daughter but answers his own questions. Once he has identified his daughter with his wife and both with whatever is possessing him, Morella reaffirms this identification with the words "'I am here!'" (2:33). The anima erupts fully and undeniably into consciousness, but the ego is so weak and shattered that it has no way of permanently assimilating it, of achieving some balance with the unconscious. The trauma is symbolically resolved with the death of the second Morella.

In Morella's third transmogrification lies a final lesson of identity. Carrying the dead body of his daughter, the narrator finds the corpse of the first Morella missing from the tomb. "Morella," though, has not completely disappeared, but has become coterminous with the all, with Schelling's ultimate sense of identity, "the night in which all cats are black": "And I kept no reckoning of time or place, and the stars of my fate faded from heaven, and therefore the earth grew dark, and its figures passed by me, like flitting shadows, and among them all I beheld only—Morella" (2:34). The anima no longer exists as a differentiated, crystallized image, but collapses, taking the ego with it, into the unconscious realm from which it emerged. This "wild Pantheism" (2:28) is a dark, perverse, regressive version of the luminous self-awareness that accompanies proper individuation, "when the bright stars become blended—into One," as envisioned at the end of *Eureka* (16:314).

A look at "Ligeia" will help fill out this anatomy of the anima and the ego's responses to it by revealing similar psychic dynamics from another angle. Like the openings of "The Assignation" and "Morella," the first sentence of "Ligeia," with its ambiguous syntax, suggests intimate associations between the title character and the narrator's own psyche or "soul": "I cannot, for my soul, remember how, when, or even precisely where, I first became acquainted with the lady Ligeia" (2:248). One of the reasons he gives for this anomaly is that her attributes made their way into his heart "by paces so steadily and stealthily progressive that they have been unnoticed and unknown" (2:248). Even her entrances into the narrator's "closed study"—and the expression is used here in a double meaning—are as gradual and elusive. "She came and departed as a shadow" (2:249). These descriptions parallel the way Poe defines intuition in *Eureka* as the apprehension of ideas that present themselves to consciousness, but have their origins deep and obscured in the unconscious.

Ligeia is presented less as a living woman than along one dimension as "an airy and spirit-lifting vision more wildly divine than the phantasies which hovered about the slumbering souls of the daughters of Delos" (2:249–50). Associations with the mysterious, the ethereal, the dreamlike and visionary pervade the narrator's description. Ligeia has "the beauty of beings either above or apart from the earth—the beauty of the fabulous Houri of the Turk" (2:251); in her chin is found "the gentleness of breadth, the softness and the majesty, the fullness and the spirituality, of the Greek—the contour which the god Apollo revealed but in a dream to Cleomenes, the son of the Athenian" (2:251). Ligeia, as we soon learn, is herself a poet, just as Morella speaks in a highly alliterative and rhythmic, elusive and allusive prose, and, in an earlier version of the story, also recites a poem.[28] Both Ligeia and Morella, then, are like Helen in that they lead into a world of mythopoeic experience, a world from which our rational egos have estranged us, but which is our birthright; they draw their partners through, as James Hillman puts it, "the constructed world of concepts and dead things into an animistic, subjective, mythical consciousness, where fantasy is alive."[29] Hillman elaborates further: "Functionally anima works as that complex which connects our usual consciousness with imagination by provoking desire or clouding us with fantasies and reveries, or deepening our reflection. She is both bridge to the imaginal and also the other side, personifying the imagination of the soul."[30]

The phrase "deepening our reflection" calls attention to a related component of the anima as the all-knowing psychopomp, the bearer of the highest philosophical wisdom. The epigraph to "Morella," for example, is originally spoken in Plato's *Symposium* by Diotima of Mantinea, the woman who reveals to Socrates himself the greater mysteries of love. As Jung says of the anima, "something strangely meaningful clings to her, a secret knowledge or hidden wisdom, which contrasts most curiously with her irrational elfin nature. . . . Rider Haggard calls She "Wisdom's Daughter"; Benoît's Queen of Atlantis has an excellent library that even contains a lost book of Plato."[31] We have already seen the range and nature of the learning of Morella, a Presburg graduate, and we can assume that Ligeia has been educated in the same Germany of the soul. The narrator speaks of the latter's "infinite supremacy" to guide him "through the chaotic world of metaphysical investigation" (2:254): "Her presence, her readings alone, rendered vividly luminous the many mysteries of the transcendentalism in which we were immersed" (2:254).

It is the nature of archetypal symbols like the anima to hold together qualities we customarily think of as opposing; so we should not be surprised to find that alongside this ethereal spirituality and vast erudition there is an intense, more closely physical desire that the narrator several times calls "wild"—what Jung describes as "the chaotic urge to life."[32] Twice, within the space of as many pages, Ligeia's husband uses almost identical words to try to describe this: "It is this wild longing—it is this eager vehemence of desire for life—*but* for life—that I have no power to portray—no utterance capable of expressing" (2:256). This wild desire is not merely for a longer existence, either before or after death, but for an expansion of vision, a deepening of experience, a widening of the boundaries of what life can be. As Jung says of the anima: "It is something that lives of itself, that makes us live; it is a life behind consciousness that cannot be completely integrated with it, but from which, on the contrary, consciousness arises."[33] In Bronson Alcott's series of "Orphic Sayings," a similar feminine entity appears, sometimes linked with "the soul" but at other times having no clear referent, and she is spoken of in terms that anticipate the tone and the vision of the end of *Eureka*: "The insatiableness of her desires is an augury of the soul's eternity. . . . She would breathe life, organize light; her hope is eternal; a never-ending, still-beginning quest of the Godhead in her own bosom."[34]

It is this vision of ultimate unity, and man's potential to become one with the One through *gnosis* and through love, that the narrators of "Morella" and "Ligeia" shrink from. This wisdom is intimated in things deep, distant, timelessly old, in certain musical sounds and in certain passages from books, but as in "Morella," its primary avenue and focal symbol is in the eyes of Ligeia: "What was it—that something more profound than the well of Democritus—which lay far within the pupils of my beloved?" (2:251). The narrator's bafflement suggests something vaguely intuited but always receding before the full grasp of consciousness or articulation, a phenomenon upon which he comments: "There is no point, among the many incomprehensible anomalies of the science of mind, more thrillingly exciting than the fact—never, I believe, noticed in the schools—that, in our endeavors to recall to memory something long forgotten, we often find ourselves *upon the very verge* of remembrance, without being able, in the end, to remember. And thus how frequently, in my intense scrutiny of Ligeia's eyes, have I felt approaching the full knowledge of their expression—felt it approaching—yet not quite be mine—and so at length entirely depart!" (2:252). It is significant that the "full knowledge" the narrator is seeking is linked, as in Whitman's "Facing West from California's Shores," with elusive memory, for indeed he had experienced the unity once at an unconscious level. His difficulties now are suggested in his very language. He talks objectively, of "the science of mind," of the "fact" he is himself experiencing. He wants the knowledge to "quite be mine," whereas the very condition for it is a degree of ego abandonment. The problems of his mode of approach are epitomized in the sentence: "Yet not the more could I define that sentiment, or analyze, or even steadily view it" (2:252). His most self-destructive stance, though, is his sense that the knowledge toward which Ligeia is leading him is beyond the sphere of the human, and that to venture beyond the ego is to infringe upon some jealous God. The narrator speaks with some hope but with more fear of "studies but little sought—but less known . . . down whose long, gorgeous, and all untrodden path, I might at length pass onward to the goal of a wisdom too divinely precious not to be forbidden!" (2:254). Jung says of the anima that "she makes us believe incredible things, that life may be lived."[35]

Immediately after these lines, in which the narrator expresses his rigidities, anxieties, and mystifications, he states that Ligeia's health began to decline; just as the knowledge she proffers is too divinely precious, so "the wild eyes blazed with a too—too glorious effulgence" (2:254 55). On her death-bed, she asks the narrator to read back to her a poem she composed that includes the stanza:

> That motley drama!—oh, be sure
>   It shall not be forgot!
> With its Phantom chased forever more,
>   By a crowd that seize it not,
> Through a circle that ever returneth in
>   To the self-same spot,
> And much of Madness and more of Sin
>   And Horror the soul of the plot.   [2:257]

The Phantom here is similar to "the ungraspable phantom of life" at the beginning of *Moby-Dick*, in whose pursuit Narcissus drowns through his naive and direct attempt at grasping.[36] The paradox that both Melville and Poe seem to be confronting is that one cannot seize the mystery of life consciously, but must allow oneself to be seized by it.

The "Conqueror Worm" who appears in the following stanza is not mere physical death, but a uroboric destroyer of consciousness. Ligeia's suggestion for finally conquering this conqueror seems to escape the narrator. Her dying words, supposedly from Joseph Glanvill but constructed by Poe himself, and iterated here for the fourth time in the course of the tale, are: *"Man doth not yield him to the angels, nor unto death utterly save only through the weakness of his feeble will"* (2:258). Yet the entire "quotation" includes the sentence "For God is but a great will pervading all things by nature of its intentness," and Ligeia also exclaims shortly before her death, "O God! . . . Are we not part and parcel in Thee?" (2:257). The occulted but higher truth of the passage seems to be that man yields himself to death by trying to assert and identify with his own feeble will instead of acceding to and rejoining the all-encompassing will beyond his ego. Poe may have taken the notion of God as a great will from Fichte's term, "Moral Will," which is synonymous with the philosopher's absolute Ego, but the subtleties of psychological delineation are Poe's own.

The narrator's ego disintegration, the result of his rejection and repression of the anima, is more rapid and more dramatic than that in "Morella." In what he calls his "mental alienation" (2:259), he turns to opium, black magic, and sadism as dark inversions of authentic ways to loosen the boundaries of the ego. Although there is little verisimilitude in any of Poe's women, the narrator's second wife, Lady Rowena Trevanion, of Tremaine, at least has a local habitation and a name, however literary both may be.[37] Compared to Ligeia, whose origins, family name, and ultimate nature are shrouded in mysteries, Rowena has a relatively independent existence, and much of the second half of the story is Poe's depiction of the mechanisms of projection on this existence, whereby unassimilated psychic elements are erroneously perceived as aspects of the outside world. As Jung writes: "Projections change the world into the replica of one's own unknown face. In the last analysis, therefore, they lead to an autoerotic or autistic condition in which one dreams a world whose reality remains forever unattainable."[38] The ending of "Ligeia," as with many Poe tales, recounts in a particularly vivid and horrifying way the return of the repressed, a consummation devoutly to be wished for and feared: "Then rushed upon me a thousand memories of Ligeia—and then came back upon my heart, with the turbulent violence of a flood, the whole of that unutterable woe with which I had regarded *her* thus enshrouded" (2:264).

D. H. Lawrence was right when he noted that Poe's great theme was the human mind "in a great continuous convulsion of disintegration."[39] But integral to this theme is a complementary vision of psychic expansion, of an extended and balanced soul in harmony with itself and the universe. In examining Poe's feminine figures, it is important to stress their potential for psychic growth as well as their actual effect of psychic dissolution. The ego itself plays the major role in its own tragedy, but it is neither compelled nor condemned to do so.

V.

THE DOUBLE

CONSCIOUSNESS

REVISITED

We have already noted some of the convergences between Emerson and Jung, convergences that are striking both in vision and in method. Both men operate from a common Romantic inheritance that emphasizes the reintegration of the mind with nature and that of the mind itself. Both view the nature of the universe and the nature of the mind as ultimately harmonious, both within themselves and with each other. Both perceive a play of opposites that have the potential to balance and reconcile each other. And both view artistic activity as a way of achieving this reconciliation and of joining the conscious with the unconscious.[1] These similarities in content are highlighted by, and to some extent the result of, similarities in approach and method. Both Emerson and Jung are deliberately unsystematic thinkers, always allowing an immediate present truth to be articulated no matter what its relationship to the overall movement of their thought, while still maintaining a confidence in the relatedness of all these momentary truths. Neither wrote a summary compendium, but tried, as Emerson describes it, "to find the journey's end in every step of the road" (3:60). Jung creates a parable on the error of valuing final results over the processes through which they were discovered,[2] and elsewhere writes: "The goal is important only as an idea; the essential thing is the *opus* which leads to the goal: *that* is the goal of a lifetime."[3]

One of the problems, then, in juxtaposing Emerson and Jung is not that they have so little in common but that they have so much. Their angles of vision are sometimes so close that new perspectives cannot be created; there is not enough imaginative and conceptual distance to construct genuinely fruitful analogies. Although a multiplication of points of contact would strengthen the theoretical framework of this study, there is a need to be selective in choosing those relationships that provide insights into the nature of the works themselves. This chapter tries to deepen the connections between Jung and Emerson by narrowing itself to the relationships between psychological dynamics and literary style and structure, particularly as seen in Emerson's essay "Experience."

A promising place to begin is the problematic issue of what Emerson calls "the double consciousness." As early as 1833, Emerson says in a sermon: "Man begins to hear a voice that fills the heavens and earth saying that God is within him. . . . I recognize the distinction of the outer and the inner self; the double consciousness that within this erring, passionate, mortal self sits a supreme, calm immortal mind, whose powers I do not know; but it is stronger than I; it is wiser than I; it never approved me in any wrong; I seek counsel of it in my doubt; I repair to it in my dangers; I pray to it in my undertakings. It seems to me the face which the creator uncovers to his child."[4] As Emerson went further in thought and experience, the relations between the two halves came to seem less clear and comfortable. In his classic statement of the problem, an 1841 journal entry, incorporated the next year in the lecture "The Transcendentalist," he writes: "The worst feature of our biography is that it is a sort of double consciousness, that the two lives of the Understanding & of the Soul which we lead, really show very little relation to each other, that they never meet & criticize each other, but one prevails now, all buzz and din, & the other prevails then, all infinitude & paradise, and with the progress of life the two discover no greater disposition to reconcile themselves."[5] This notion of the double consciousness is used by Emerson in a number of contexts, and has been interpreted by critics in even more varied ways.[6] From our discussion so far, however, it may be helpful to make a tentative alignment of Emerson's "inner self" or "Soul" and its "infinitude & paradise" with Plato's Asia of the mind, and the "Understanding" and its "buzz and din" with the analytic intellect of Europe. This strategy also suggests a linking of the former with the "general consciousness" of *Eureka* and the "primal thought" of "Passage to India," and the latter with the "individual consciousness" and the restless, feverish progeny of Adam and Eve. In more explicitly psychological terms, the Soul, or, as Emerson also calls it, the Reason, and the Understanding correspond to the dual centers of the psyche, the self and the ego.[7] Such a configuration does not simply reduce a basically ontological problem to subjectivism, but follows the contours of Emerson's own development, moving from theological doctrine to a more general phenomenology of mind. Stephen Whicher describes the direction of Emerson's thought in the 1830s: "The rock on which he based his life was the knowledge that the soul of man does not merely, as had long been taught, contain a spark or drop or breath or voice of God; it is God. . . . No sooner does the discovery of God at the heart of the self heal the division of God and man, than self splits in two, and the old submission to an objective God is repeated within the sphere of the subjective."[8]

The problem, then, can be viewed as that of finding an appropriate and viable relationship between the God within and the man within. Once the ego separates itself from "the ocean of love and power, before form, before will, before knowledge" (4:62), how does it deal with the resulting sense of anxiety and isolation? If the separation is too complete and abrupt, the anxiety and isolation bordering on despair, the condition can be termed—to use a worn word, but one that has a precise meaning in analytical psychology—"alienation."[9] The ego experiences the rest of the self as radically Other; the division set out at the beginning of Emerson's first book, *Nature*, between the *me* and the *not-me* (1:4–5), runs through the psyche itself. As Emerson writes, contrasting his desire and his faith with his experience: "A believer in Unity, a seer of Unity, I yet behold two."[10] Often this sense of alienation emerges in images of deprivation in the midst of plenitude, of the pervading proximity of the inaccessible. More specifically, we are often placed immediately on the shore of the ocean of love and power, which always recedes before our Tantalus touch. In "The Poet," Emerson writes: "The fate of the poor shepherd, who, blinded and lost in the snow-storm, perishes in a drift within a few feet of his cottage door, is an emblem of the state of man. On the brink of the waters of life and truth, we are miserably dying" (3:33). And in "Experience," he says that people "stand on the brink of the ocean of thought and power, but they never take the single step that would bring them there" (3:56–57). Though this attitude is not Emerson's permanent habitation, it is another version of the problem of the double consciousness, of the gap between the Understanding and the Soul, with the speaker standing on the limited and limiting side of the chasm, as suggested by the adverbs: "*now,* all buzz and din . . . *then,* all infinitude and paradise."

An opposite danger awaits, though, on the other side of the chasm. The double consciousness can be collapsed into a condition that has been called "inflation,"[11] where the ego confounds its own aims and powers with those of the entire psyche. The process can result in an unrealistic aggrandizement of the ego and in a sense of power not fully apprehended or controlled. Perhaps one of the reasons that Emerson's transparent eyeball passage in *Nature* is such an easy target of satiric and critical deflation[12] is that it suggests this hazardous identification of the ego with the self: "Standing on the bare ground,—my head bathed by the blithe air and uplifted into infinite space,—all mean egotism vanishes. I become a transparent eyeball; I am nothing; I see all; the currents of the Universal Being circulate through me; I am part or parcel of God" (1:10). After we are told that all mean egotism vanishes, we encounter a sentence in which the pronoun "I" occurs four times. And though one of its contexts is explicitly self-negating—"I am nothing"—the statement is difficult to reconcile with a head uplifted into infinite space. The I-eye pun seems only to underscore these difficulties rather than to create insight.

Further, without leaning too hard on the image, we can note that a transparent eyeball would, of course, see nothing, because light would pass directly through it. Emerson, like some of Poe's narrators, seems to want it both ways here, to plug into the currents of the Universal Being without modifying the structure or the strength of the ego.

The problems here, however, may have less to do with the nature of Emerson's actual experience, which is inaccessible to us anyway, than with the language that seeks to express and create it. Emerson himself speaks to the difficulties involved when he writes: "Language overstates. Statements of the infinite are usually felt to be unjust to the finite, and blasphemous. Empedocles undoubtedly spoke a truth of thought, when he said, 'I am God;' but the moment it was out of his mouth it became a lie to the ear. . . . How can I hope for better hap in my attempts to enunciate spiritual facts?" (1:198–99). Elsewhere, he says: "The waters of the great deep have ingress and egress to the soul. But if I speak, I define, I confine and am less" (2:342). His most succinct and famous pronouncement on the problem is: "There is no doctrine of the Reason which will bear to be taught by the Understanding" (1:129).

The problem of the double consciousness, then, proliferates. The ontological and psychological impinges on the linguistic. The search for a viable relation, a "disposition to reconcile" the Soul and the Understanding, is also a search for a medium, a redeeming language through which there can be commerce between the two. We have seen in Chapter 1 how, theoretically at least, the conception of the symbol in Emerson and Jung can provide such a bridge. And yet in the actual structure of a literary work, which necessarily moves in time, a static symbol or mandala is difficult to create and is often ineffective. There is an analogy here to psychic development: one cannot in reality try to maintain some kind of golden mean between alienation and inflation, because, as painful or distorting as they might be, they are necessary for psychic growth. Edward Edinger, using a visual metaphor we have already encountered in Hawthorne, maintains that repeated alternations between the two, each movement accompanied by an increment in awareness and integration, are at the heart of the individuation process: "The process of alternation between ego-Self union and ego-Self separation seems to occur repeatedly throughout the life of the individual both in childhood and in maturity. Indeed, this cyclic (or better, spiral) formula seems to express the basic process of psychological development from birth to death."[13]

Viewed from this perspective, the problem of the double consciousness moves towards its own solution, as Emerson came to see. Toward the end of a relatively late essay, "Fate," he writes: "One key, one solution to the mysteries of human condition, one solution to the old knots of fate, freedom, and foreknowledge, exists; the propounding, namely, of the double consciousness. A man must ride alternately on the horses of his private and his public nature, as the equestrians in the circus throw themselves nimbly from horse to horse, or plant one foot on the back of one and the other foot on the back of the other" (6:47). In the context of this essay, the double consciousness clearly comes to embrace other dualisms related to the Understanding and the Reason, such as freedom and fate, form and power, mind and nature. The imagery here, though, gives us a more specific sense both of these dualities and of the dialectics used to reconcile them. The symbol of a rider and his horses has reverberations at least as far back as Plato's *Phaedrus* with the control of the intellect over the rest of the psyche and body. In "The Poet," Emerson keeps part of the same vehicle, but asks us to reverse our stance toward the tenor: "As the traveller who has lost his way throws his reins on his horse's neck and trusts to the instinct of the animal to find his road, so we must do with the divine animal who carries us through the world" (3:27). In the passage from "Fate," however, Emerson suggests a relation between the extremes of dominance and abandonment. The circus rider must be acutely sensitive and responsive to the movements of the horses without yielding completely to the movements—by offsetting them himself by just the right amount. He must be in constant motion, aware of the differences between himself and the horses, yet fusing them all into harmonious interaction. It is, paradoxically, the movement itself that gives balance, stability.

Thomas Weiskel has observed that "any aesthetic . . . becomes or implies a psychology,"[14] and certainly the converse is equally true. The implications for aesthetics are anticipated by Emerson in a passage from "Plato": "Every great artist has been such by synthesis. Our strength is transitional, alternating; or, shall I say, a thread of two strands. The sea-shore, sea seen from shore, shore seen from sea; the taste of two metals in contact; and our enlarged powers at the approach and at the departure of a friend; the experience of poetic creativeness, which is not found in staying at home, nor yet in travelling, but in transitions from one to the other, which must therefore be adroitly managed to present as much transitional surface as possible" (4:55–56). The imagery and movement of the prose here reflect both equestrian stances: jumping from one horse to another and keeping one foot on each horse. The first laconic and abstract statement is explained by the second, the latter part of which is a concrete image that restores a tactile quality to the earlier word "strength." The rest of the passage is a series of correspondences, moving from the concrete to the abstract, from the grammatically simple to the grammatically complex, without ever itself completing a syntactical sentence. The alliterative and onomatopoeic unfolding of "sea-shore"—"sea seen from shore, shore seen from sea"—makes us aware that the word describes not so much a thing in itself as a boundary between two opposites that is also their meeting place. Possible engulfment in the ocean is put in dynamic balance with the solidity of the shore through the chiasmus. The echoing "t" sounds both between "taste" and "two" and within "taste" and "contact" reinforce the sense of joining in the gustatory metaphor. And the preponderance of function words, especially prepositions, toward the end of the last "sentence" emphasizes the transitional movement and surface.

These strategies of multiple perspective, continuous transition, and ever-renewing dialectic are the foundations of Jungian individuation as well as Emersonian art. Whitmont writes that the therapeutic situation in analytical psychology "involves a mutual recognition of limitations and boundaries which, at the same time, are points of encounter, where the partners touch. . . . Every problem 'solved' constellates a new problem. The conversation between unconscious and consciousness, between Self and ego, between God—infinite life—and finite man, never ceases."[15] One way of viewing Emerson's works is to see this conversation taking place within the discourse itself, as in this famous paragraph from "Circles": "Our moods do not believe in each other. To-day I am full of thoughts and can write what I please. I see no reason why I should not have the same thought, the same power of expression, to-morrow. What I write, whilst I write it, seems the most natural thing in the world; but yesterday I saw a dreary vacuity in this direction in which now I see so much; and a month hence, I doubt not, I shall wonder who he was that wrote so many continuous pages. Alas for this infirm faith, this will not strenuous, this vast ebb of a vast flow! I am God in nature; I am a weed by the wall." (2:306–7). The sentences increase in length to the pivotal fourth sentence, with its crucial "but," and then decrease. As we move from sentence to sentence we encounter the important technique of chiasmus, here not so much of syntax as of thought. The fourth sentence begins, as the ones before it, in the present, a moment of fullness and power; but changes tenses to look back toward an infertile past and forward to a discontinuous future. The following sentence reverses this position by talking about "*this* infirm faith . . . *this* vast ebb of a vast flow," as if the apparently immediate moment of strength and contact has already been transformed into the future promised in the previous utterance. The stance is again reversed in the very last sentence: the logic of parallelism may require the first clause to come last, but this is also the logic of stasis, of form inhibiting power. The tide now turns in each sentence, as the paragraph reaches its climax.

Indeed, this last sentence—"I am God in nature; I am a weed by the wall"—can serve as a microcosm of the Emersonian aesthetic. If these words had appeared in a poem by Whitman, one could argue that the two parts merely say the same thing in different ways. But particularly in the context of this essay and this paragraph, the parallel structure of the halves underscores the disparity in viewpoint, the distance between inflation and alienation. The injunction to "present as much transitional surface as possible" seems to be violated by the presence of only a stark semicolon. Yet this makes the issue of transition even more obtrusive; the reader is forced to focus on how to move between the two clauses. He must circle back to the first sentence of the paragraph and to the movement of the entire essay for clues. What is elliptical at one point is often elaborated at another. As James Cox writes: "The connections we have to make to discover the full sequence are by no means free association; they are the fated spatial silences between the sentences, instinct with implicit energy—dots, we might say, which when connected form the circle of the essay."[16]

The implicit energy and the satisfaction of connecting the dots come from the fact that the discontinuities and leaps are not merely rhetorical or logical but reflect the psychological dynamics we have been exploring. One of Emerson's key insights is that we speak at different times from different areas of the psyche. Any single moment, any single utterance is necessarily fragmentary. In "Nominalist and Realist," Emerson writes: "As much as a man is a whole, so is he also a part; and it were partial not to see it" (3:236). Later in the same essay, Emerson's techniques of chiasmus and contradiction threaten to fragment the discourse into complete chaos: "No sentence will hold the whole truth, and the only way in which we can be just, is by giving ourselves the lie; Speech is better than silence; silence is better than speech;—All things are in contact; every atom has a sphere of repulsion;— Things are, and are not, at the same time;—and the like. All the universe over, there is but one thing, this old Two-Face, creator-creature, mind-matter, right-wrong, of which any proposition may be affirmed or denied" (3:245).

A test of Emerson's much-disputed sense of humor might be the degree to which he is aware of the self-satire here. But though at times, as here, these insights undermine and inhibit their very expression, at other times, as in "Experience," Emerson is able to turn them into triumph.[17] Characteristically and appropriately, "Experience" discusses its own method only after we have moved through virtually all of it, searching for the connections and transitions that will help us follow its dizzying circlings and reversals. A sentence toward the end, "I gossip for my hour concerning the eternal politics" (3:83), suggests the uneasy situation of a speaker bound to time and form dealing with that which is beyond form. The tension between "gossip" and "eternal" recalls the sense of double consciousness that pervades the essay. And yet the phrase "eternal politics" itself implies that the latter realm is not without its divisions, its opposition parties, its threads of relation to the quotidian.

In a more general way, the essay succeeds because Emerson raises our awareness of the force and limitations of each utterance and of the intricate relations among them: "Illusion, Temperament, Succession, Surface, Surprise, Reality, Subjectiveness,— these are threads on the loom of time, these are the lords of life. I dare not assume to give their order, but I name them as I find them in my way. I know better than to claim any completeness for my picture. I am a fragment, and this is a fragment of me" (3:82–83). Emerson is not saying that these topics and their order are random and haphazard, but that they are more discovered than invented or imposed by an over-controlling ego unaware of its own limits. Indeed, although each of these sections contains within itself its own qualifications and alternations, the entire essay does follow a discernible but zigzag course from the most alienated position of the ego toward the ultimate mysteries of the self and back out to the periphery of the psyche. Although still a "fragment" at the end of the essay, the speaker is not merely back where he began but has moved closer to that state where "the soul attains her due sphericity" (3:80). The essay not only presents the results of its exploration, but is constructed to simulate the process itself, "the imaginative graph of the experience which the artist lived in the course of his journey to knowledge."[18]

The Illusion of the opening section is not as much misconception as an almost impenetrable distance from the source. The beginning question, "Where do we find ourselves?" (3:45), is not as much answered as reemphasized in the second sentence: "In a series of which we do not know the extremes, and believe that it has none" (3:45). The simile "We are like millers on the lower levels of a stream, when the factories above them have exhausted the water" (3:46) brings to mind an image we have already encountered in Emerson, "that unknown country in which all the rivers of our knowledge have their fountains" (12:30). A similar image from "The Over-Soul"—"Man is a stream whose source is hidden. Our being is descending into us from we know not whence" (2:268)—suggests that Emerson is describing a state of psychic alienation, of the ego cut off from both its origins and its goals. The constant elusiveness of the genuine, the "perpetual retreating" like the horizon (3:46), the "evanescence and lubricity of all objects" (3:49) recall Poe's narrator always being on the verge of the knowledge Ligeia represents.

By contrast, Temperament seems to offer some permanency and authenticity and may prove to be "the iron wire" that connects moment to fragmentary moment, step to step. But temperament is as restricting as it is apparently constant, and "also enters fully into the system of illusions and shuts us in a prison of glass which we cannot see" (3:51–52). Although in this section we are deeper into the essential being of the person, Temperament is still a relatively superficial and overestimated aspect of the psyche that must be reckoned with on its own level, but ultimately transcended by more central and more transpersonal powers: "Into every intelligence there is a door which is never closed, through which the creator passes. The intellect, seeker of absolute truth, or the heart, lover of absolute good, intervenes for our succor, and at one whisper of these high powers we awake from ineffectual struggles with this nightmare" (3:54–55).

The beginning of the next section, on Succession, explains why the essay does not—and perhaps cannot—move directly to these absolutes: "Our love of the real draws us to permanence, but health of body consists in circulation, and sanity of mind in variety or facility of association" (3:55). This anticipates the dialectic delineated in "Plato," between unity and variety, being and becoming. In one sense, the former terms seem "the real," the more basic, as when Emerson suggests in this section why the story that pleased the child yesterday does not today: "Because thou wert born to a whole and this story is a particular" (3:56). But the very rhetorical context—both immediately (this statement is prefaced by "But will it answer thy question to say. . . ?" [3:56]) and in large—reminds us that this is a fragment of a fragment, this very statement of potential wholeness. Indeed, it is only through these partialities that the whole can be rediscovered. The paradox is epitomized in the last sentence of the section: "Like a bird which alights nowhere, but hops perpetually from bough to bough, is the Power which abides in no man and in no woman, but for a moment speaks from this one, and for another moment from that one" (3:58). Emerson, master of the concise and epigrammatic, gives us a sprawling sentence filled with balanced and seemingly redundant phrases. The tension between Power as a kind of static absolute—and this is the only time the word is capitalized in the fifteen occurrences in the essay—and as the very embodiment of flux, distributed through a succession of prepositional phrases, is difficult for the mind to hold together.

We are relieved then, in the next section, on Surface, to be told bluntly that "life is not dialectics" (3:58). This section is the most quoted and quotable of the essay, and is read by some as signaling a major reorientation in Emerson's development.[19] Its emphasis on moderation—"The mid-world is best" (3:64)—and anti- or at least nonintellectualism—"Intellectual tasting of life will not supersede muscular activity" (3:58)—has found responsive souls both in Emerson's America and in ours. We must not forget, however, that this is itself only the mid-section of the seven divisions, and that in Emerson's work and in this essay particularly, a statement can be positive and persuasive and still be provisional: "Speak what you think now in hard words and to-morrow speak what to-morrow thinks in hard words again, though it contradict every thing you said to-day" (2:57). We have entered far enough into the workings of the essay to realize that this very concern with surface implies what is beyond or beneath it.

A vivid example of this technique is the transition between

Surface, with its line "A man is a golden impossibility" (3:66), suggesting at once Aristotle's Golden Mean and the difficulties rather than the ease of moderation, and the next section, Surprise, which begins "How easily, if fate would suffer it, we might keep forever these beautiful limits . . ." (3:67). For no sooner do we give our assent to the joys and the values of the day-to-day, to the ability of consciousness to determine the kind of life it can make for us, than we are told that power "keeps quite another road than the turnpikes of choice and will; namely the subterranean and invisible channels of life" (3:67). Surprise—as the famous lines from "Merlin," where the poet will "mount to paradise / By the stairway of surprise" (9:107), and as the structure of "Experience" suggest—is the means by which we pass from Surface to Reality, and it can serve as well as any word to describe the Emersonian aesthetics of perpetual transition: "Nature hates calculators; her methods are saltatory and impulsive. Man lives by pulses; our organic movements are such; and the chemical and ethereal agents are undulatory and alternate; and the mind goes antagonizing on, and never prospers but by fits" (3:68). Surprise is the Emersonian equivalent of ecstasy, where the painfully constructed ego is abandoned for the ever-new fullness of the self. The section ends with the words "the individual is always mistaken. It turns out somewhat new and very unlike what he promised himself" (3:70).

This is particularly helpful advice in reading the next section, Reality, because "that which is coexistent, or ejaculated from a deeper cause, as yet far from being conscious, knows not its own tendency. . . . Bear with these distractions, with this coetaneous growth of the parts; they will one day be *members*, and obey one will" (3:70). Here, if anywhere, we would expect to come, in the words of Thoreau, "to a hard bottom and rocks in place, which we can call *reality*, and say, This is, and no mistake."[20] But an essential part of Emerson's Reality, of the nature of the self, is the same attribute we saw in the very first section, its ultimate elusiveness and irreducibility to verbal or conceptual containers. "Underneath the inharmonious and trivial particulars, is a musical perfection; the Ideal journeying always with us, the heaven without rent or seam" (3:71). But it would be a presumptuous inflation for the ego to think it can bind to itself this joy, either in words or in experience: "Every insight from this realm of thought is felt as initial, and promises a sequel. I do not make it; I arrive there, and behold what was there already" (3:71). The Reality is inexhaustible and fluid: "Suffice it for the joy of the universe that we have not arrived at a wall, but at interminable oceans" (3:73). And this is still the sea seen from the shore. After listing the "quaint names, too narrow to cover this unbounded substance" (3:72), Emerson himself can call it only a name that is so abstract and subsuming as to not be a name, "Being, and thereby confess that we have arrived as far as we can go" (3:73).

Part of the genius of the essay is that it does not end here, but returns us from "the great and crescive self, rooted in absolute nature" (3:77), to an enlarged ego that must finally assimilate part of what it has encountered and return to speak it. This is the ineluctability of Subjectiveness, which—although it brings us back to some of the distortions of Illusion and Temperament—preserves our humanity. There is no erasing the discovery we have made that we exist, but we can better understand the limitations and implications of the situation: "We have learned that we do not see directly, but mediately, and that we have no means of correcting these colored and distorting lenses" (3:75). This section closes with a reassertion of the permanence and impermeability of the double consciousness that the rest of the essay has qualified and to some extent undermined: "In Flaxman's drawing of the Eumenides of Aeschylus, Orestes supplicates Apollo.... The face of the god expresses a shade of regret and compassion, but is calm with the conviction of the irreconcilableness of the two spheres. He is born into other politics, into the eternal and beautiful. The man at his feet asks for his interest in turmoils of the earth, into which his nature cannot enter" (3:82). Without trying to mitigate the force and poignancy of this vision, we must point out that still the god is part of us, or rather, we are part of the god. As Emerson reminds us in the same essay: "The consciousness in each man is a sliding scale, which identifies him now with the First Cause, and now with the flesh of his body; life above life, in infinite degrees" (3:72). The section after the semi-colon may appear to be a characteristic Emersonian chiasmus in that the First Cause should be the element closest to "life above life, in infinite degrees." But what the phrase really refers to is the entire sliding scale, on which man is condemned to be *now* at one point, *now* at another. "I can very confidently announce one or another law, which throws itself into relief and form, but I am too young yet by some ages to compile a code" (3:83). The double consciousness, then, remains at the heart of Emerson's percep-tion. His art can neither avoid it nor completely transcend it, but it can engage and realize it. If it is indeed wisdom to find the journey's end in every step of the road, then for Emerson, as for Whitman, that road is endless and open.

VI.

WORDS OUT OF

THE SEA:

WALT WHITMAN

In a notebook dated 1847, Walt Whitman wrote: "I cannot understand the mystery, but I am always conscious of myself as two—as my soul and I: and I reckon it is the same with all men and women."[1] The poetry Walt Whitman later was to write depicts with a particular vividness and immediacy the double consciousness that we have seen in Emerson and in this prose entry. The songs often tramp a perpetual journey between a sense of the presence and fullness of the entire self and of a consciousness painfully alienated from its deepest sources, as we see in microcosm in the following lines:

> Behold the great rondure, the cohesion of all, how perfect!
> But as for me, for you, the irresistible sea is to separate us. . . .
> [107]

One of the dramatic crosscurrents in Whitman's greatest poem, "Song of Myself," is the continuous dialectic between "the Me myself" (32) mentioned in section four—"Apart from the pulling and hauling stands what I am, / Stands amused, complacent, compassionating, idle, unitary" (32)—and the multiplex buzz and din that surrounds, fragments, invades, delights, diffuses that self. In some of the poems, the paradigm of unity-division-reintegration can be viewed beyond this dialectic, not as a pattern inexorably controlling every line, but as a way of achieving perspective on what might otherwise seem aimless vacillations. As Whitman writes in one of the "Inscriptions" to *Leaves of Grass*:

> Ever the dim beginning,
> Ever the growth, the rounding of the circle,
> Ever the summit and the merge at last, (to surely
> start again,) . . .   [5]

This chapter examines in some detail three of these poems: "Chanting the Square Deific" fits almost too neatly, as if the pattern were a template for its creation; "The Sleepers" relates to the pattern more shaggily, but some of its impenetrability can be nudged back by our framework; and "Out of the Cradle Endlessly Rocking" implies the pattern but at the same time dramatizes the difficulties in enacting it.

Despite the prodigious efforts of scholars like Floyd Stovall, we cannot be sure of the extent of Whitman's knowledge of the occulted traditions that shaped American Romanticism,[2] but it is almost certain that he knew something of them, at least through indirect and somewhat dubious sources.[3] However much he knew consciously of previous uses of the quaternity figure—the *tetraktys* of the Pythagoreans, the Gnostic figure of the Barbelo (God is Four), and the *quaternio* of alchemy—there is no reason to doubt that this knowledge fused with unconscious factors to produce a powerful symbol of wholeness in "Chanting the Square Deific." As Whitman said in conversation: "It would be hard to give the idea mathematical expression: the idea of spiritual equity—the north, south, east, west of the constituted universe (even the soul universe)—the four sides as sustaining the universe (the supernatural something): this is not the poem but the idea back of the poem or below the poem. I am lame enough trying to explain it in other words—the idea seems to fit its own words better than mine. You see, at the time the poem wrote itself: now I am trying to write it."[4] Although we have to suspect some conscious shaping and artistic crafting on Whitman's part, a juxtaposition of the poem with Jung's analysis of the quaternity symbol supports Whitman's suggestion that the poem arose from sources beyond the intellect.[5]

As with the paradigm, the poem begins with the One:

> Chanting the square deific, out of the One advancing,
>   out of the sides,
> Out of the old and new, out of the square entirely divine,
> Solid, four-sided, (all sides needed,) from this side
>   Jehovah am I. . . .   [443]

We note immediately the balance struck between the square's unfolding, dynamic nature—emphasized by the use of present participles and the quadruple repetition of "out of"—and its nature as a completed construct—"solid," "four-sided." "Four-sided" is, of course, redundant modifying "square," but this tautology stresses what we are to keep constantly in mind as we view each side separately: "(all sides needed)." The Father, Jehovah-Brahm-Saturnius, is apparently the first to emerge from the One, yet in elementary ways he simply is the One in its aboriginal, unrealized state, containing within itself opposites before they differentiate. Just as the One is "old and new," the Father is also "old, modern as any," dispensing laws "aged beyond computation, yet ever new" (443). In executing these laws, the Father seems to lack an element not only of human responsiveness but even of volition, because the judgments are as blind and automatic as the laws of nature. Indeed, the Father is the psychic equivalent of nature, "that objective spirit," as Jung puts it, "which today we call the unconscious: it is refractory like matter, mysterious and elusive, and obeys laws which are so non-human or suprahuman that they seem to us like a *crimen laesae majestatis humanae.*"[6] Other phrases in this first section—"the Earth," "the brown old Kronos" (443)—reinforce the association with that dark, preconscious, unhumanized realm in which the ego begins to crystallize.

The next side, the Consolator, suggests this crucial development, growing out from the Father but moving in a radically different direction. Christ-Hermes-Hercules provides the missing elements of will and human sympathy. He tempers law with mercy and affection, and takes upon himself other human emotions such as sorrow. This second triad of mythic figures may seem incongruous, linking the mild and compassionate with the almost brutally heroic, but Whitman seems to have intuited what Jung makes explicit, that the essential meaning of heroism is the victory of the conscious over the unconscious.[7] The three figures Whitman mentions all have the capacity to descend into the underworld and return intact. Jung refers to "the long-hoped-for and expected triumph" of consciousness,[8] and Whitman's Consolator is "the promis'd one," "Foretold by prophets and poets in their most rapt prophecies and poems" (444). But this god, like the Father, is only partial and requires a complementary opposite to realize its very being. Just as the Father could become such only by incarnating or splitting off a Son, so the Son is good only if it can confront an evil equally powerful and real, not just the *privatio boni*. Whitman stresses this point by calling the third side, Satan, "equal with any, real as any" (445). Jung writes: "Once the indefinable One unfolds into two, it becomes something definite: the man Jesus, the Son and Logos. This statement is possible only by virtue of something else than is *not* Jesus, not Son or Logos. The act of love embodied in the Son is counterbalanced by Lucifer's denial."[9] In other words, any development within the unified psyche creates differentiation; one cannot split a whole and have only a part remain. Whitman's Satan partakes of some of the remaining aspects of the first side, the ignorance and darkness, but is primarily a distinct and separated principle. He is "a drudge," "brother of slaves," "with sudra face" (444), and despite his own pride and defiance in this role, he does the work of physical necessity. Jung argues that the trinity is an incomplete symbol because it denies or ignores the importance and inexorableness of the body, of material existence: "We can only rise above nature if somebody else carries the weight of the earth for us. What sort of philosophy would Plato have produced had he been his own house-slave? . . . The dark weight of the earth must enter into the picture of the whole. In 'this world' there is no good without its bad, no day without its night, no summer without its winter."[10] Whitman's inclusion of Satan as an equal and real side of his deity contrasts with the basically elitist and repressive nature of any philosophy or religion that aspires to complete spirituality.

But this inclusion of "warlike" (445) Satan creates a conflict situation that can be resolved, in turn, only by a symbol that moves the opposition to a plane beyond that of direct confrontation. Such a symbol is the fourth side of the Square Deific.

> Santa Spirita, breather, life,
> Beyond the light, lighter than light,
> Beyond the flames of hell, joyous, leaping easily above hell,
> Beyond Paradise, perfumed solely with mine own perfume,
> Including all life on earth, touching, including God,
>   including Saviour and Satan,
> Ethereal, pervading all, (for without me what were all?
>   what were God?)
> Essence of forms, life of the real identities, permanent,
>   positive, (namely the unseen,)
> Life of the great round world, the sun and stars, and of man,
>   I, the general soul,
> Here the square finishing, the solid, I the most solid,
> Breathe my breath also through these songs.   [445]

The speaker who is "Beyond Paradise" recalls the voice in Emerson's "Brahma" that says "Find me, and turn thy back on heaven" (9:171). The wholeness includes and transcends the dualities of heaven and hell, good and evil, the spiritual and the earthly. "Saviour" and "Satan" are linked not only by symbol, but by syntax and alliteration. This fourth side is at once ethereal, a breath, a light beyond light, and "solid." Santa Spirita, in completing the square, returns us to the point of origin, but "the Earth," "the brown old Kronos" (443), has been transmuted into the "life of the great round world" (445), infused by an incandescence that suggests a psychic reunion in which ego awareness reaches out to include that which lies beyond it. Jung describes the Holy Ghost in the quaternity context as "a reconciling light in the darkness of man's mind, secretly bringing order into the chaos of his soul. The Holy Ghost is like the Father, a mute, eternal, unfathomable One in whom God's love and God's terribleness come together in wordless union. And through this union the original meaning of the still-unconscious Father-world is restored and brought within the scope of human experience and reflection."[11] Whitman's Santa Spirita, of course, is not wordless, and like Psyche in Poe's "To Helen" is feminine, complementing, harmonizing, and subsuming the three preceding masculine sides.

Still, Jung's analysis of the quaternity can stand as a helpful gloss on a poem he had apparently never read. When the figure is understood in its full significance, "it can no longer be doubted, either, that a common life unites not only the Father with the 'light' son, but the Father and his *dark* emanation. The unspeakable conflict posited by duality resolves itself in a fourth principle which restores the unity of the first in its full development. The rhythm is built up in three steps, but the resultant symbol is a quaternity."[12] These three steps correspond to the pattern of unity, differentiation, and restored harmony that is imbedded in Romantic thought and in Jung's theory of individuation. It would be both simplistic and presumptuous, however, to infer that Whitman had achieved individuation in 1865, when this poem was written, or was at this point more in harmony with himself than at other times. This study has avoided making direct correlations between the texts and the lives and psychic conditions of the authors, not because the connections are not there, but because they are oblique, tortuous, and usually beyond the scope of the literary critic. We have *Leaves of Grass* before us as a concrete, living reality, but "Walt Whitman" the person is in comparison a ghost, an abstraction, a construct patched together out of shreds of evidence. An even greater difficulty is a sort of psychic Heisenberg Indeterminacy Principle. To take the present example, is this symbol of wholeness thrown up from the unconscious as a compensatory reaction to a divisive civil war and whatever personal turbulences Whitman was experiencing,[13] or does it evince a psyche already well on the way back to "Reconciliation" (321), the title of another poem written in the same year? In other words, to what extent does the very writing of the poem alter the emotional conditions from which it arose?

A failure to confront these complexities mars Harry Cook's notion that any interpretation of Whitman's poetry must in large part be autobiographical, and that "The Sleepers" "reflects the psychic individuation process which resulted in Whitman's ability to write poetry."[14] His comments about the poem itself, however, suggest profitable avenues for the interpreter: "Structurally the poem goes through an implied cyclical process: implied innocence or oneness, psychic fragmentation, despair, and then a unifying process."[15] Although archetypal psychology cannot explicate every detail or movement of this intractable and deliberately elusive poem, it can help us with general perspectives and with some of the imagery and transitions. One of the reasons critics have had special problems with this dream vision is that they often take the dream as a distortion or jumbled recombination of more "real" daytime experiences. From the point of view of James Hillman, by contrast, the dream brings us into direct touch with psychic realities unfiltered by an often tyrannizing and falsifying ego consciousness. Hillman's position is an appropriate prolegomenon to a reading of "The Sleepers" on its own terms:

> Dreams are important to the soul not for the messages the
> ego takes from them, not for recovered memories or reve-
> lations; what does seem to matter to the soul is the nightly
> encounter with a plurality of shades in an underworld, as
> if dreams prepared for death, the freeing of the soul from its
> identity with the ego and the waking state. It has often been
> said that in dreams the soul "wanders," which means not
> literal walking through the world but leaving the confines
> of the ego's concerns. In dreams the fragmentation into parts
> is held together by scenes and woven into stories. What
> we learn from dreams is what psychic nature really is—
> the nature of psychic reality; not I, but we; not one, but
> many. Not monotheistic consciousness looking down from

the mountain, but polytheistic consciousness wandering all over the place. . . .[16]

"The Sleepers" begins:

I wander all night in my vision,
Stepping with light feet, swiftly and noiselessly stepping and stopping,
Bending with open eyes over the shut eyes of sleepers,
Wandering and confused, lost to myself, ill-assorted, contradictory,
Pausing, gazing, bending, and stopping.   [424]

Perhaps because this is not a dream but a poetic simulation of one, we are led into it by the ego, the "I" of the first line, who is here the only center of sight and consciousness, all others sleeping with shut eyes. This ego, though, soon becomes "lost to myself": the repetitions of "stepping" and "stopping" reinforce the confusing, hesitant, backtracking motions, the ambiguity of reference taking on more importance as the poem proceeds—the adjectives and participles seem at first to refer only to "I," but as this "I" later fuses into and out of "night" and "my vision" we cannot be sure. The first image—the quiet, sleeping infants—seems more like what the conscious would expect and hope the unconscious to be like—dormant, lulled, powerless, comforting. A little lower layer reveals, however, images such as "the white features of corpses," "the gash'd bodies on battlefields" (424). As horrid as they might be, these images are of a transitional nature, representing, as Hillman suggests, the movement from the physical to the psychical, where "something material is losing its substance and thrust,"[17] as indeed happens when "the night pervades and infolds them" (424), and the subsequent images become paired, loving, ordered. The last image in this series, the mother "sleeping with her little child carefully wrapt" (425), echoes the more general infolding process of night, suggesting as yet implicit connections between the two. The train of associations, then, takes a turn in identifying sleep with permanent loss of the senses, confinement, flight, and finally death itself. An "I" soon reenters for the first time since line one, and despite the meandering motions undergoes a progression of transformations. The "I" at first only passes his hands close to the sleepers without touching. He then changes to one who can "sleep close" (425) to the other sleepers, and moves to one who dreams "all the dreams of the other dreamers" and has even "become the other dreamers" (426). The "I" then becomes movement itself: "I am a dance—play up there! the fit is whirling me fast!" (426). Finally, the "I" dissolves into a uroboric realm that precedes even the most elemental kinds of separation and creation: "Cache and cache again deep in the ground and sea, and where it is neither ground nor sea" (426).

This is regression not in the service of the ego but in the service of the self. From the viewpoint of the daytime ego, the movement is perceived correctly as disorienting pathology, but in the world of dream and art, it is an alternative way of being and experiencing. As Hillman writes: "Schizoid polycentricity is a style of consciousness and not only a disease; and this style thrives in plural meanings, in cryptic double-talk, in escaping definitions, in not taking heroic committed stances, in ambisexuality."[18] We should not look, then, for the kinds of rational explications we can make of some other poetry, but if anything, for the psychologic behind double-talk such as "I reckon I am their boss and they make me a pet besides" (426). The ego's relation to other parts of the psyche is now constantly in flux; he is by turns their leader and follower, their butt and boss in confused revelry, and the music they march to is crazed but sometimes strikingly melodic: "Onward we move, a gay gang of blackguards! with mirth-shouting music and wild-flapping pennants of joy!" (426). The erratic but dense patterns of alliteration and assonance move the line sprawlingly forward until the aural surprise of the last word, which unlike the other nouns and adjectives, carries over no preceding sound.

The exuberant eroticism implicit here emerges fully and powerfully towards the end of this first section.

I am she who adorn'd herself and folded her hair expectantly,
My truant lover has come, and it is dark.

Double yourself and receive me darkness,
Receive me and my lover too, he will not let me go
    without him.

I roll myself upon you as upon a bed, I resign myself
    to the dusk.

He whom I call answers me and takes the place of my lover.
He rises with me silently from the bed.

Darkness, you are gentler than my lover, his flesh was
    sweaty and panting,
I feel the hot moisture yet that he left me.

My hands are spread forth, I pass them in all directions,
I would sound up the shadowy shore to which you
    are journeying.   [426–27]

To view these lines primarily as masturbatory or homosexual wish-fulfillment fantasies is to give tacit assent to the ego-centered notion that dream and poetry are secondary, peripheral, or substitute experiences.[19] This is an experience in itself, linking eroticism with ego transcendence, a link that will be explored in more detail in the next chapter. For now, a quotation from Georges Bataille will be helpful: "The transition from the normal state to that of erotic desire presupposes a partial dissolution of the person as he exists in the realm of discontinuity. Dissolution— this expression corresponds with *dissolute life*, the familiar phrase linked with erotic activity. The passive, female side is essentially the one that is dissolved as a separate entity. But for the male partner the dissolution of the passive partner means only one thing: it is paving the way for a fusion where both are mingled, attaining at length the same degree of dissolution."[20] If we take these notions intrapsychically, as we certainly should to avoid oversimplified distinctions between men and women, we can see that the pronomial chaos and other ambiguities in this section are deliberate and crucial. A line like "I roll myself upon you as upon a bed, I resign myself to the dusk," through both image and the balanced rhythm, enacts a shift or interaction between the masculine active and the feminine passive.[21] The receptivity, splitting, engulfment, penetration, and dissolution recapitulate all the stances and relations that the "I" has taken toward the darkness up to this point. That the vision here is more reciprocal and mutual than in some of the previous imagery, with maternal and incestuous overtones such as burrowing and being infolded, though, suggests a movement away from uroboric immersion. The "I," however elusive it now is, meets the darkness on more equal terms, and becomes enriched and expanded through the joining of the feminine and the masculine that the darkness has mediated and itself partaken in.

The opening lines of the next section—"I descend my western course, my sinews are flaccid, / Perfume and youth course through me and I am their wake" (427)—suggest at once postcoital relaxation, "the little death," and an accompaniment of night on its diurnal course around the globe. "Wake" takes on a double meaning as the "I" then identifies with images of old age, bereavement, and finally death itself—"A shroud I see and I am the shroud" (427)—suggesting an even deeper identification with darkness and the underworld as the "I" becomes itself that which infolds and envelops. And yet despite—or because of—this identification, the "I" has now had enough, or too much, of this draining, enervating existence, and as a way of extricating himself makes the vapid and suspect statement: "It is dark here under ground, it is not evil or pain here, it is blank here, for reasons" (427). The following four sections, then, take the form of more structured, coherent, unified narratives in clearer language, although their import and relationships to each other are as enigmatical as the rest of the poem.

The "beautiful gigantic swimmer swimming naked" (428) of section three resembles the brilliant fictional creation of Walt Whitman in "Song of Myself," that thirty-seven year old kosmos, who goes "undisguised and naked" (29) and wills the reader "to be a bold swimmer" (84). The poem that came to be titled "The

Sleepers" appears as the fourth in the original 1855 *Leaves of Grass*, and it is natural that the now dislocated, fragmented, and exhausted "I" would turn to the presiding spirit of that volume in search of a tenable identity. But it is important that this figure be ultimately rejected and superseded for further expansion and perception, as he himself realizes at the end of "Song of Myself": "I effuse my flesh in eddies, and drift it in lacy jags" (89). These dispersing and dismembering eddies reappear four times in this short section of "The Sleepers," resembling the whirling dance that diffuses identity in section one (426), as Mutlu Blasing has pointed out.[22] Though the apparent defeat by the battering and swirling sea is viewed as tragic, it is also a necessity for the poet, who, as Shakespeare was reported to have said of Mercutio, was forced to kill this character "to prevent being killed by him."[23] A central difficulty for the artist is that any one symbol is transcended and superannuated by the living and perpetual flux of the psyche; Whitman confronts the possibility elsewhere "that before all my arrogant poems the real Me stands yet untouch'd, untold, altogether unreached" (254).

But whether it is this symbol itself, or the very act of writing, or the darkness that the "I" cannot extricate himself from at the beginning of the next section is unclear. "I turn but do not extricate myself, / Confused, a past-reading, another, but with darkness yet" (428). Knowing whether the "yet" has the force of "still" or of "but" would help us determine if the "darkness" here mitigates or adds to the confusion, but this matter itself is left confused. The syntax does suggest that this scene is another "past-reading," suggestive of some of the tableaux in "Song of Myself" and also of the diffusion and multiplication of the gigantic swimmer. Each of these middle four scenes has a self-dissolving quality, and the "I" seems increasingly to accept this flux and flow: he hates the swift eddies that kill the single swimmer; he rushes to the scene of the shipwreck, but is powerless and helps to pick up the dead without further comment. He does not even appear in the double tableaux of Washington or in the story of the squaw who never reappears; in the latter it seems to be only his mother who grieves for and is fixated on the loss.

It is not that the "I" has inured itself to human sympathy, but that he already intuits the reappearance in section seven of "the beautiful lost swimmer," "the red squaw," and many of the other figures previously mentioned—the criminal, the stammerer, and, of particular significance, the actor and actress whose very nature it is to take on other personalities (431). The vision of merger and movement, of being all and still faintly and obscurely one, is recaptured at a higher level here.

> Elements merge in the night, ships make tacks in
>   the dreams,
> The sailor sails, the exile returns home,
> The fugitive returns unharm'd, the immigrant is back
>   beyond months and years . . .   [430]

This is less regressive than the mergers at the very beginning of the poem, for the elements still retain their identities in the very act of return and reunion: "The diverse shall be no less diverse, but they shall flow and unite—they unite now" (432). What the "I" has brought back from his night wanderings is what Hillman calls "a new connection with multiplicity" in which "we would find ourselves no longer alone in our subjectivity. Our possessive notion of ownness, our privative notion of privacy—the private self—indeed the very notion of the unit as the basis for the fantasy of ourselves, would no longer provide the model on which our house of splinters is built."[24]

Hillman's point about transcending subjectivity is crucial for us. Near the beginning of this study it was suggested that there is a link between the dynamics and structure of "Passage to India" and that of "The Sleepers." It would be too easy a mistake simply to take the former as objective and the latter as subjective, and read the Anacharsis Clootz congregation of nationalities that follows the three lines quoted above as merely figurative. For each of the poems can be seen as crossing the same bridge in different directions: "Passage to India" moving from the external, technological, societal to the psychic possibilities now available through these factors; "The Sleepers" moving so deeply into the self as to go beyond what we normally think of as its bounds into a transpersonal substratum. As Jung says about the effect of dream: "It is not our ego-consciousness reflecting on itself; rather, it turns its attention to the objective actuality of the dream as a communication or message from the unconscious, unitary soul of humanity."[25] A quotation from Emerson can both underscore this convergence of Jung and Whitman and suggest that dream is one context where the double consciousness is not the problem but the solution: "My dreams are not me; they are not Nature, or the Not-me: they are both. They have a double consciousness, at once sub- or ob-jective. . . . We are let by this experience into the high region of Cause, and acquainted with the identity of very unlike-seeming effects" (10:13–14). For all three men, there is a basic unity in which all people share when they are freest from external disguises and conscious constraints:

> The sleepers are very beautiful as they lie unclothed,
> They flow hand in hand over the whole earth from east to
>   west as they lie unclothed,
> The Asiatic and African are hand in hand, the European
>   and American are hand in hand. . . .   [432]

The movement here from east to west, from Asia to America, anticipates that in "Facing West from California's Shores" and "Passage to India," suggesting the closing of the circle. The very ending of the poem makes clear, though, that what is achieved by the "I" is not a steady and static state of individuation, but a recognition of the need and value of the kinds of descents and ascents the poem depicts.

> I too pass from the night,
> I stay a while away O night, but I return to you again
>   and love you. . . .
>
> I will stop only a time with the night, and rise betimes,
> I will duly pass the day O my mother, and duly return to you.
>   [433]

Like the ships making tacks, the "I" must move through a
zigzag journey, knowing when to flow with and when against the
winds and currents. "Out of the Cradle Endlessly Rocking" suggests how urgent yet perilous these returns to the mother, the
night, the darkness are. The first section, a single long sentence
originally separated from the rest of the poem as a "Pre-Verse,"
seems to epitomize the three states, but the predominant vantage
point here, as in the entire poem, is that of the second, the newly
separated ego, with longing and questioning glances at what it
has left and what may come.

> Out of the cradle endlessly rocking,
> Out of the mocking-bird's throat, the musical shuttle,
> Out of the Ninth-month midnight,
> Over the sterile sands and the fields beyond, where the child
>   leaving his bed wander'd alone, bareheaded, barefoot,
> Down from the shower'd halo,
> Up from the mystic play of shadows twining and twisting
>   as if they were alive,
> Out from the patches of briers and blackberries,
> From the memories of the bird that chanted to me, . . .
> A man, yet by these tears a little boy again,
> Throwing myself on the sand, confronting the waves,
> I, chanter of pains and joys, uniter of here and hereafter,
> Taking all hints to use them, but swiftly leaping
>   beyond them,
> A reminiscence sing.   [246–47]

Some of the critics of the poem see the first few lines as depicting the birth experience itself,[26] and point to what was originally
the third line—"Out of the boy's mother's womb, and from the
nipples of her breasts"[27]—as evidence of the primal physicality
of the experience. Whitman's later excision of this line, however, may have less to do with suppression or sublimation than
with the sense that biological birth is primarily a metonymy here
for the birth of consciousness, the initial separation of the ego

from the rest of the psyche. As Neumann writes: "The 'round' of mythology is also called the womb and uterus, though this place of origin should not be taken concretely. In fact, all mythology says over and over again that this womb is an image, the woman's womb being only a partial aspect of the primordial symbol of the place of origin."[28] Whitman's portrayal of this realm, accordingly, includes several related images: the uroboric, eternal ocean, the psychic state of sleep, nature becoming musical—and later even articulate—through the throat of a bird, the synesthetic interweaving mesh created by a "shuttle"—later echoed in "shadows twining and twisting"—and the beginning, fruition, and endpoints of the annual and diurnal cycles, "the Ninth month midnight." The journey "over the sterile sands" describes the separation from this fertile and sustaining but also enveloping and encompassing world. That the child is "bareheaded, barefoot," intensifies the fact that he is now "alone," vulnerable and exposed. As the long sentence moves forward, the differentiating opposites that accompany growing ego awareness appear: "*Down* from the shower'd halo, / *Up* from the mystic play of shadows. . . ." The "fitful risings and fallings" (247) are clearly related to the endlessly rocking sea, but the separation now into flow and ebb, the advance and retreat of each wave, emphasizes the dualistic nature of the process. The late risen moon is half dark and half light.

The speaker is, then, in Emerson's terms, reenacting the fall of man, making the discovery that he exists. The emphasized, anaphoric prepositions "out of'" and "from" have a double valence: the dark, unitary realm is one "out of'" and "from" which the poet finds his words, but it is also one which the poet has to be removed "from" and "out of" in order to be a poet, to utter them. The paradox is embodied in the physical position of being on the sand, but "confronting the waves," the sea seen from shore. A related paradox, more extensively developed in the rest of the poem, is that the speaker can move toward repairing the fall, toward healing the split, through his very songs of separation, of "yearning and love" (247); he envisions reconciling "pains and joys," uniting "here and hereafter," integrating the halfway world of a child's inchoate ego with the consciousness of an adult. This double perspective—"A man, yet by these tears a little boy again"—is vital for the poem, for the enhancement and insight work both ways: the early experiences shape later emotions and developments, but these later interactions add significance and coherence to the childhood events. Louise Kaplan, a psychologist who has done research on early childhood from a psychoanalytic perspective, expresses well this mutual and reciprocal relationship that goes beyond developmental determinism: "The complex behaviors of an adult can never be reduced to their infantile origins. . . . By the time we reach adulthood the blunt passions of infancy have been enriched and transformed many times over. Our adult actions are but distant echoes, distorted reflections, metaphorical paraphrases of the events of our second birth. Even so, adulthood is not the end of childhood or the completion of a journey that goes only forward. The maturing adult is continually reliving and revising his memories of childhood, refinding his identity, reforging the shape of his selfhood, discovering new facets of his being."[29] The poet's backward glance, then, is not solely a regressive activity, for the hope is that this circuitous night-sea journey through the past will bring a future expansion of self.

The drama that unfolds in the rest of the poem details and extends this vision at the same time it undermines any hope of easy and uncomplicated victory. The reminiscence itself begins with a mockingbird who enjoys a state of union with his mate analogous to the uroboric realm that the child is moving out of and from.

> *Two together!*
> *Winds blow south, or winds blow north,*
> *Day come white, or night come black,*
> *Home, or rivers and mountains from home,*
> *Singing all time, minding no time,*
> *While we two keep together.*   [248]

The mockingbird obviously has some awareness of the oppositions
he articulates, but these differentiations of circumstance, time,
and place have little relevance to his state of being—*"Singing all
time, minding no time."* The interweavings of sounds—"two together," "white/night"—and the symmetries and echoings across
caesuras emphasize the paradisal harmony of this world.

It is significant, however, for the overall tenor of the poem that
the mockingbird is given nine lines to sing his bliss as opposed to
sixty-two for lament and grief. In this lament, the elements of the
world assume a new separateness—the mockingbird addresses,
in turn, the winds, moon, land, stars, sea—and yet all are colored
by the pervasiveness of absence: *"Whichever way I turn, O I think
you could give me my mate back again if you only would"* (250).
This creature of nature now experiences himself as alienated
from the harmonious, comforting aspects of the natural world:

> *Close on its wave soothes the wave behind,*
> *And again another behind embracing and lapping,*
> *every one close,*
> *But my love soothes not me, not me.* [249]

A poignant irony here, intentional on the part of the poet-man, is
that the bird's song itself is even more melodic and moving than
when the birds were *"two together!"* The embracing, rhythmic
movements of the world are perceived and articulated even more
keenly from the viewpoint of one's own separation. The lament is
more resonant, evocative, because as true symbols the images and
sounds conjure, suggest, try to grasp that which is not there—not
only the she-bird herself, but the oneness of being they enjoyed
together.

Related to this, but even more important than the bird's aria, is
the response of the boy who becomes the poet through "peering,
absorbing, translating" (248). Before the main part of the lament,
the boy is pictured as still partially submerged in the uroboric
realm of mute darkness: "For more than once dimly down to the
beach gliding, / Silent, avoiding the moonbeams, blending myself
with the shadows" (249). After hearing the lament, the boy rejects

or is rejected by the silence, the harmony, the peace of this realm: "For I, that was a child, my tongue's use sleeping, now I have heard you, / Now in a moment I know what I am for, I awake" (251–52). He never again wants "to be the peaceful child I was before what there in the night" (252). This single awakening clearly compresses and symbolizes a series of experiences, insights, movements toward growth; and the bird's song is more a correlative than a cause of the boy's discoveries, all involving the increasing independence of the ego and its separation from the all within and without. The bare feet and head reappear in a context of exultation: "The boy ecstatic, with his bare feet the waves, with his hair the atmosphere dallying" (251). The boy is touching the waves and the air, but that very touch stresses his boundaries, his separateness from them; he is dallying, flirting, as with another. He can say, along with the speaker in "Song of Myself" although in a different context: "Is this then a touch? quivering me to a new identity?" (57).

This realization, then, produces ecstasy as well as despair, for it awakens and intensifies the possibilities for love. When the ego is still under the powerful sway of the rest of the psyche, it is fully aware neither of its own existence nor of the distance between it and what surrounds it. And without this perceived distance, this otherness, this discontinuity between the *me* and the *not-me*, there can be no genuine yearning and no authentic love. One of the reasons Emerson ultimately rejects a monistic idealism in *Nature* is the lack of distinctions, of an "I" and a "Thou": "It leaves me in the splendid labyrinth of my perceptions, to wander without end. Then the heart resists it, because it balks the affections in denying substantive being to men and women" (1:63). For the speaker in "Out of the Cradle," the foreshortened and dramatically compressed separation of the ego is indeed a parting that is such sweet sorrow, releasing and realizing stirrings that were incipient and unfocused.

Never more the cries of unsatisfied love be absent from me . . .
The messenger there arous'd, the fire, the sweet hell within,
The unknown want, the destiny of me.   [252]

And yet this very moment of isolation, of initiation into the conditions of being "a single separate person" (1), is at the same time a moment of communion. The speaker asks of the bird: "Is it indeed toward your mate you sing? or is it really to me?" (251). Although the bird himself is unaware of it, his unanswered, unrequited plaint has been comprehended, absorbed, and perpetuated by another singer whose relation to his audience is not as unsuspecting: "O you singer solitary, singing by yourself, projecting me, / O solitary me listening, never more shall I cease perpetuating you" (252). The bird's mate, the boy's envelopment, are on one level gone forever. But because the very experience of ego separation is universal, an authentic and effective symbolization of the process will be a bridge not only back inward but out toward others, awakening from them in turn "A thousand warbling echoes . . . the thousand responsive songs" (252–53). The kind of love voiced in "Out of the Cradle" must be by its very conditions unsatisfied, but this does not preclude some kinds of completions and fulfillments. In the "Calamus" poems, Whitman writes:

> Sometimes with one I love I fill myself with rage for fear
>   I effuse unreturn'd love,
> But now I think there is no unreturn'd love, the pay is certain
>   one way or another,
> (I loved a certain person ardently and my love was not
>   return'd,
> Yet out of that I have written these songs.)   [134]

A basic impulse behind Whitman's poetry is the hope, in Hawthorne's words, that "the printed book, thrown at large on the wide world, were certain to find out the divided segment of the writer's own nature, and complete his circle of existence by bringing him into communion with it."[30] But Hawthorne uses these words skeptically, and even in the context of Whitman's work it would be granting too much to the poetic process to say that it can heal all the rifts and pains of the alienated ego. The closing movements of "Out of the Cradle" are not so much comforting and fulfilling as desperate and urgent in the search for these qualities. One must agree with Richard Chase that the ambivalence of phrases such as "the white arms out in the breakers tirelessly tossing" (249) and "the savage old mother" (251) cannot be totally encompassed by some kind of mystic fusion.[31]

"Death," the word the sea whispers, is in part an intimation of completed harmony, a sign that the impulse to merge does have a goal. But to seek that goal prematurely, when the newly separated or partially regressing ego can more easily be overpowered by the unconscious, is to risk annihilation, as the "I" of "The Sleepers" at several points intuits. Similarly, the psychic explorer journeying back through his past, even in the service of individuation, risks moving too far back, reentering the uroboric realm too deeply. That the speaker in "Out of the Cradle" comes treacherously close at the end to uroboric incest is suggested by the fact that death appears "low and delicious" (252). The hypnagogic repetition of the word is perceived as gently washing over his passive being:

> Creeping thence steadily up to my ears and laving me
> softly all over,
> Death, death, death, death, death.   [253]

The eroticism here seems similar to that at the end of section one of "The Sleepers," but in the latter the active is joined with the passive, the sexuality including both desire and climax, joining and release. The end of "Out of the Cradle," as suggested by the imagery and the emotional texture of the poem that follows it, "As I Ebb'd with the Ocean of Life," implies the nostalgic surrender that Neumann calls "uroboric incest." In this condition, "the emphasis upon pleasure and love is in no sense active, it is more a desire to be dissolved and absorbed; passively one lets oneself be taken, sinks into the pleroma, melts away in the ocean of pleasure—a *Liebestod*. The Great Mother takes the little child back into herself, and always over uroboric incest there stand the insignia of death, signifying final dissolution in union with the Mother."[32]

The speaker, however, does not yield himself completely to these impulses: he maintains that he will "conquer" (252) the word, and he still views the sea and its utterance as distinctly other: "Hissing melodious, neither like the bird nor like my arous'd child's heart" (253). What is delicately portrayed here is the dilemma of a poet who sees that he could most easily end his anguishing isolation through a surrender that would silence him again. As long as "death" remains a word, though, he can confront it, for through his reminiscence he is able to realize, in the ambiguous syntax of the last line, that the sea whispered "me" (253). Like the "I" of "The Sleepers" and the speaker in many of Dickinson's poems, the poet here can still envision ways in which the sea, darkness, death can breathe their breath also through his songs without dissolving the initial and hard-won separation that made him originally a poet.

VII.

KORA IN HEAVEN:

EMILY DICKINSON

As stressed throughout this study, the ultimate test of a critical approach must be practical, and the poetry of Emily Dickinson still presents the critic with basic practical problems, such as what an individual poem is "about." With increasingly more accurate and more extensive historical and biographical knowledge,[1] the relationship between the life and the work remains problematical, as much of a riddle. Though analyses of specific poems and groups of poems proliferate, the divergences and disagreements overshadow any kind of consensus.[2] The most promising direction—and this remains a proposition to be supported by the rest of this chapter rather than an initial axiom—lies in using the Romantic and Jungian theory of the psyche as a middle term between the cultural and the personal on the one hand, and the immediacy and universality of the work of art on the other.[3]

We can begin to test this hypothesis by plunging immediately into a specific crux, a disagreement between two Dickinson scholars over the interpretation of a key poem.

Wild Nights—Wild Nights!
Were I with thee

Wild Nights should be
Our luxury!

Futile—the Winds—
To a Heart in port—
Done with the Compass—
Done with the Chart!

Rowing in Eden—
Ah, the Sea!
Might I but moor—Tonight—
In Thee!   [249]

Thomas Johnson says that this is "manifestly erotic poetry" that
uses "sexual imagery with unabashed frankness."[4] Ruth Miller,
on the other hand, finds unsubstantiated Johnson's contention
that the poem "can be construed as an allegory of sexual intercourse," and offers instead the suggestion "that 'Wild Nights' may
be read simply as a variant of the idea of arrival in Heaven."[5] It
would take us too far afield to recount the details of this quarrel,
but it is interesting to note that what Miller quotes as Johnson's
analysis of "Wild Nights" is actually his analysis of the related
poem 368. The main point, however, is that neither Johnson nor
Miller is wrong, but that they each give only a partial view of the
poem. Although Miller provides impressive support for her view
from Emily Dickinson's "Lexicon"—her constantly used editon of
Webster's—her wish to deny or neglect an erotic component leads
to a reading that is not consistent even with itself: "'Moor' is 'To
confine or secure a ship in a particular station, beneath the water.
A ship is never said to be *moored* when she rides by a single
anchor.' Her heart in port is to be free of that torment of pulling
through that roadstead where her boat is weighed down by that
single anchor, the attachment to life, just outside the harbor.
Were she moored in that harbor such wild nights would be unnecessary. Fixed there with the cables and chains of security,
placid in Eden, she would not need any chart (no shoals) or any
compass (no traveling)."[6] It is difficult to see where Miller finds
the image of "placid in Eden," as the poem reads "Rowing in

Eden," a strenuous and rhythmic activity. Moreover, the first stanza tells us that nights with "Thee"—whom Miller views as God or Jesus—would be "Wild," not placid.

To acknowledge these difficulties, one would have to postulate a "heaven" that is other than conventional. Miller seems to have done to Dickinson what Jowett was accused of in connection with Plato's dialogues, of translating them into Christianity. In doing so, Miller makes the dubious bargain of exchanging deeply felt individual symbols for their lowest common denotations. Moreover, even if such a reading were accurate, it would not really explain the poem itself, because Christianity does not exist on any absolute or irreducible level of truth, but is only one set of symbologies created by the human psyche. If "Thee" means Christ, we would still want to know what "Christ" means. And to suggest, even as tactfully and cautiously as Johnson does, that the "Thee" is Charles Wadsworth, may add an undertone to the poem, but does not greatly clarify its meaning. The most useful critical statement is that of Albert Gelpi: "Her point is that love was for her an experience that had something to do with man and something to do with God: the masculine 'other' filling what her female nature lacked, ached for, and, at the same time, feared."[7]

Gelpi, though, stresses the aspect of longing and wish fulfillment, which is clearly present but coexists with a sense of ecstasy achieved in the very utterance of the words. As Gelpi recognizes in his chapter on Whitman, a poem need not be a sublimation or substitute for experience, or an abstraction from it, but can be an experience in itself.[8] The rhythmic iterations, the intricate and playful counterpointing of the long "i" and "e" assonances throughout the poem, the near-rhyme of "port" and "chart" unobtrusively completed through the internal rhyming with "Heart" help make "Tonight"—another internal rhyme—as much an impending or present reality as a subjunctive possibility. In another poem, Dickinson writes: "Exultation is the going / Of an inland soul to sea" (76), and the stress should be at least as much on "the going" as on any arrival. Elsewhere, she writes: "So instead of getting to Heaven, at last— / I'm going, all along" (324).

The basic debate over "Wild Nights" reappears in divergent

readings of other important poems, such as:

> He fumbles at your Soul
> As Players at the Keys
> Before they drop full Music on—
> He stuns you by degrees—
> Prepares your brittle Nature
> For the Etherial Blow
> By fainter Hammers—further heard—
> Then nearer—Then so slow
> Your Breath has time to straighten—
> Your Brain—to bubble Cool—
> Deals—One—imperial—Thunderbolt—
> That scalps your naked Soul—
>
> When Winds take Forests in their Paws—
> The Universe—is still— [315]

Here Thomas Johnson is on the other side of the argument, agreeing with R. P. Blackmur[9] that the He of the poem is a preacher,[10] while Clark Griffith says: "To say that these lines merely imply intercourse is to miss the point, for actually they go much further. There is an orgiastic quality about them which converts the whole poem into something monstrous and almost obscene. It is a poem which has masculine lechery for its subject, and one which seems based, in the last analysis, upon nothing more mild than the fear of impending rape."[11] That good readers can arrive at such opposing readings of this poem may say more about our general cultural biases than about the enigmatic nature of the poetry. For in this poem, as in "Wild Nights," the spiritual and the sexual are inextricably woven together and are part of the same emotional experience. The recipient of the actions is the "Soul," but the actions themselves are vividly physical; this fusion is underlined by startling juxtapositions in adjective-noun pairings, such as "Etherial Blow" and "naked Soul."

It would be a mistake, then, to view the relations between the physical and the spiritual, the sexual and the religious, as merely figurative, and to try to sort out tenor from vehicle. Although John Donne's poetry is deeply felt and brilliantly crafted, there is little disagreement in separating the religious from the secular poems, although each borrows metaphors from the sphere of the other. Emily Dickinson's poetry, by contrast, seems to emerge from a realm that is prior to such distinctions, similar to the Bengalese lyrics where Rādhā, a village girl, sings to Krishna, who is both her lover and God, "The moon has shone upon me, / the face of my beloved / O night of joy."[12] W. B. Yeats was later to write of this same Bengalese poetic tradition: "We had not known that we loved God, hardly it may be, that we believed in Him; yet looking backward upon our life we discover . . . in that mysterious claim that we have made, unavailingly, on the women that we have loved, the emotion that created this insidious sweetness."[13] Yeats writes about having this insight in retrospect, but Emily Dickinson extraordinarily incorporates it into the fabric of her verse. Not that she would have made discursive statements about the relationship of eroticism to the religious experience, but her poems are symbols in the sense stressed throughout this study, where apparently irreconcilable opposites are linked by moving to a deeper psychic level. As Kerényi writes, these symbols can be viewed as "comprehensive ideas" that "can combine very different things, such as marriage and death. . . . Mythological ideas are like the compact buds of such connections. They always contain *more* than the non-mythological mind could conceive."[14] Indeed, the very combination Kerényi mentions, marriage and death, can be said to be the mythological idea in an important group of Dickinson poems. This becomes more apparent as we set beside the first poem discussed in this chapter a comment from the letters: "Dying is a wild Night and a new Road."[15]

To explore this notion further, we can turn to three poems where the image of Death as a suitor is more explicitly worked out.

> Because I could not stop for Death—
> He kindly stopped for me—

The Carriage held but just Ourselves
And Immortality.

We slowly drove—He knew no haste
And I had put away
My labor and my leisure too,
For His Civility—

We passed the School, where Children strove
At Recess—in the Ring—
We passed the Fields of Gazing Grain—
We passed the Setting Sun—

Or rather—He passed Us—
The Dews drew quivering and chill—
For only Gossamer, my Gown—
My Tippet—only Tulle—

We paused before a House that seemed
A Swelling of the Ground—
The Roof was scarcely visible—
The Cornice—in the Ground—

Since then—'tis Centuries—and yet
Feels shorter than the Day
I first surmised the Horses Heads
Were toward Eternity—   [712]

It was a quiet way—
He asked if I was his—
I made no answer of the Tongue
But answer of the Eyes—
And then He bore me on
Before this mortal noise
With swiftness, as of Chariots
And distance, as of Wheels.
This World did drop away
As Acres from the feet
Of one that leaneth from Balloon

Upon an Ether street.
The Gulf behind was not,
The Continents were new—
Eternity it was before
Eternity was due.
No seasons were to us—
It was not Night nor Morn—
But Sunrise stopped upon the place
And fastened it in Dawn.   [1053]

Death is the supple Suitor
That wins at last—
It is a stealthy Wooing
Conducted first
By pallid innuendoes
And dim approach
But brave at last with Bugles
And a bisected Coach
It bears away in triumph
To Troth unknown
And Kinsmen as divulgeless
As throngs of Down—   [1445]

There are certain similarities among the suitors in these poems
that create a distinctive, though at the same time deliberately
shadowy and elusive, character. He is not the conventional figure
of the ghastly, wizened Grim Reaper; instead he brings to mind
the words of Edgar in *King Lear*: "The prince of darkness is a
gentleman." There is, as the speaker in the first poem says, a certain "civility" about him, an accommodating concern that makes
him "kindly" stop for her. The adjective means also "naturally,"
in the course of things, as grain ripens and suns set, but there is
an additional resonance of propriety and stateliness, especially in
the line "We slowly drove—He knew no haste," where the long
vowel assonances, the preponderance of accented monosyllabic
words, and the prominent caesura seem to slow up time itself. The

second poem reinforces these effects by portraying a figure whose demure taciturnity is founded on a sense of his own majesty, power, and authority. As in the first, a radical change in quality and perspective of consciousness is depicted. In "Death is the supple Suitor," the equivalence is made explicit in the first line, and also an undercurrent that is almost subliminal in the first two poems becomes evident: something terrifying, deceptive, sinister may lie behind the courtly, considerate exterior. Most of the adjectives, however, that contribute to this impression—"stealthy," "pallid," and "unknown," just as "quivering and chill" in the first poem—do not modify directly the figure himself, so there is no direct accusation, only suggestion. The last two lines imply comfort, but also the muffling of consciousness, and the variant "And Pageants as impassive / As Porcelain" is even more frightening, with its image of cold, hard blankness.

An earlier poem can be used to supplement this composite picture of death.

Dust is the only Secret—
Death, the only One
You cannot find out all about
In his "native town."

Nobody knew "his Father"—
Never was a Boy—
Had'nt any playmates,
Or "Early history"—

Industrious! Laconic!
Punctual! Sedate!
Bold as a Brigand!
Stiller than a Fleet!

Builds, like a Bird, too!
Christ robs the Nest—
Robin after Robin
Smuggled to Rest!   [153]

For each of the attributes mentioned in the third stanza, we can find either direct verbal echoes or other corroboration in the three other poems. "Industrious" foreshadows the persistence and diligence of the supple suitor, the long patient trips he continually makes; "Laconic" his "quiet way," and the divulgelessness of his "Kinsmen"; "punctual," his prompt but "kindly" call for the first speaker, herself still unready; "Sedate," his civil, unrushed bearing, his initial "dim approach." "Bold as a Brigand" anticipates his stealth and deceptiveness, as well as his "brave at last" knowledge of final and certain victory. The variant for "Stiller" in the fourth line of the stanza is "Swifter," perhaps a better choice, as the former overlaps with "Laconic and Sedate," although there is also the remoter resonance of lurking always in wait. "Swifter" foreshadows the "swiftness, as of chariots," the dramatic yet silent way the speaker of the second poem is transported. The syntax of this third stanza, the use of a series of abstract adjectives without any referent within the stanza, reinforces the amorphous, obscured, inscrutable nature of the figure depicted in the first two stanzas. The imagery and elliptical syntax of the fourth stanza make it unclear whether Christ, also a robber and smuggler, is in league with this figure, opposed to him, or identical with him—one a disguise for the other. Is the "Nest," like the "House" in the first poem, a potentially permanent place of rest, or a honeymoon stop, intermediate between life and something else? This poem, then, restores depth and significance to the worn notion of Death as the Great Unknown. All four poems maintain the mysterious and unfathomable nature of death, while at the same time deal with the very real emotions that can exist *about* death. And these emotions are directly related to the Great Unknown within the mind, the rest of the self. As Jung says, "The immediate meaning of 'immortality' is simply a psychic activity that transcends the limits of consciousness. 'Beyond the grave,' or 'on the other side of death' means, psychologically, 'beyond consciousness.' "[16]

One wishes Jung himself had gone beyond this "simply," but fortunately a later analytical psychologist, Rosemary Gordon, has dealt with the implications and nuances in "The Death Instinct and Its Relation to the Self."[17] In her analysis, the basic direction of the ego is toward the separation and differentiation needed for a personal existence, whereas the urge toward fusion and unity may be either regressive or integrative, a slide back into uroboric unconsciousness or a healing of the split. Feelings about death and dying can be associated with this urge toward fusion, which is, although we may not experience it to be so, as much a part of the psyche as more ego-directed faculties. Along with the capacity to separate off is "the faculty to be in a state of non-being, of death—at least in approximation to it—to experience it through fantasy and through symbols; to feel it, to wish for it, to sense it. In the nightly withdrawal from consciousness we have a partial death. The revving up of an aircraft, which then through the momentum of its speed breaks through the bonds of the earth's gravity, may give one the experience of death—of being all and nothing, no longer a person carried by a plane, but oneself plane, speed, and space."[18] It is interesting to see how close the specific example of a plane's takeoff is to the imagery of being carried off suddenly in "This World did drop away," but more importantly and more generally, this theory provides us with a way of viewing Dickinson's fascination with death as not necessarily morbid or pathological:

> It is possible that a person's attitude to death depends upon what may be tentatively called his position on a wholeness-separateness axis. This is to say, a person who has invested his emotions in the experience of separateness and identity, that is, in the ego and its functions—such as sensations, reason, reality testing, and personal achievement—such a person will regard death as the enemy—the thief, the raper, the ruthless destroyer; for death will take from him all that he values. But the person whose needs are primarily directed towards synthesis and wholeness and towards lessening tensions may look on death as a liberator, a lover, a bringer of peace.[19]

Because everyone feels pulls toward both ends of this axis to some degree, we can respond to the ambivalence we have noted in Dickinson's poems, of viewing death as both a gentleman and a robber, a liberator and a destroyer. Moreover, these formulations help us to see how an attraction toward death can reflect a deeper urge toward individuation. Jung writes that "the highest summit of life can be expressed through the symbolism of death . . . for any growing beyond oneself means death."[20]

Death, in the poems we are examining, is a messenger of the self in the same way that we have seen Helen, Morella, and Ligeia to be. They each offer a person of the opposite sex the possibilities of psychic transformation or destruction. The unknown, the non-ego, can either be incorporated within consciousness to some extent or can overpower it completely. Dickinson's poems and Poe's works capture both the terrors of the ego as its limits are being transcended and its ecstatic visions of what lies beyond. The "Troth unknown" (1445) can become either the chill extinction of night hinted at in the words "The Dews drew quivering" (712) or the sudden, dazzling, and permanent illumination of consciousness where "Sunrise stopped upon the place / And Fastened it in Dawn" (1053), that "Rendezvous of Light" she describes in a poem (1564) ending a letter on the early death of her nephew: "—his Requiem ecstasy—Dawn and Meridian in one."[21] Death is like night in another poem, "a gay unknown / Whose Pomps allur and spurn / And dower and deprive" (1675).

Rosemary Gordon concludes her own explorations with some thoughts that help us see better why and how death is a suitor and a lover in the Dickinson poems: "Basic to the experience of love is an aversion to separation. Thus the drive for union, here described as the death instinct, plays an important part. And, indeed, the most intense expression of love, orgasm, is often experienced and described as a death-like state, as a loss of boundary, of identity; there is a merging with the loved object, or a merging with the loved object into some even greater unit."[22] Further, Georges Bataille writes, in what can be a gloss on the striking phrase "naked Soul" (315): "Stripping naked is the decisive action. Nakedness offers a contrast to self-possession, to discontinuous existence, in other words. It is a state of communication revealing a quest for possible continuance of being beyond the confines of the self."[23]

To pursue these connections between death and love, we can examine another poem where the male figure is deliberately left indefinite, where aspects of a human lover, of death, of God are incorporated.

> To my small Hearth His fire came—
> And all my House aglow
> Did fan and rock with sudden light—
> 'Twas Sunrise—'twas the Sky—
>
> Impanelled from no Summer brief—
> With limit of Decay—
> 'Twas Noon—without the News of Night—
> Nay, Nature, it was Day—   [638]

On one level, this poem describes the experience of orgasm: the motions of fanning and rocking, the rhythmic regularity and repetition of sounds and constructions, the intense activity in a small central place spreading throughout the entire house/body. The habit of interpreting all objects as sexual symbols can make us miss the intensity and force when a genuinely effective and appropriate sexual metaphor occurs, as here. The fire imagery provides a bridge between eroticism and death, as is suggested by the various uses of the word "consummation," and by the comment of Gaston Bachelard: "Fire suggests the desire to change, to speed up the passage of time, to bring all of life to its conclusion, to its hereafter . . . it magnifies human destiny; it links the small to the great, the hearth to the volcano."[24] The very movement of the first stanza, from the "small Hearth" to the whole house to sunrise and the sky embodies this sense of transformation from the domestic to the cosmic, from the ego to the all. The abruptness of this change is emphasized by the phrase "with sudden light," and it is this very suddenness that poses a danger to the survival of the ego, as suggested in the last stanza of another poem:

> And if I gain! Oh Gun at Sea!
> Oh Bells, that in the Steeples be!
> At first, repeat it slow!

For Heaven is a different thing,
Conjectured, and waked sudden in—
And might extinguish me!   [172]

Elsewhere, she asks Eden to "come Slowly," lest, like "the fainting
Bee," she be overpowered and "lost in Balms" (211). The image is
powerful and revealing: the bee, the buzzing, active, apparently
intelligent creature can be smotheringly surfeited and encompassed by the object of desire. Similarly, at the end of another
poem, Dickinson wonders if "It might be easier / To fail—with
Land in Sight— / Than gain—My Blue Peninsula— / To perish—
of Delight" (405).

In "To my small Hearth," however, the "sudden" is followed by
"light," suggesting that the ego has survived the encounter and is
able to perceive and exist in the new realm. Indeed, this realm is
not completely new, because it is similar to the undifferentiated
state before consciousness, where, as Neumann says, "day and
night, yesterday and tomorrow, genesis and decay . . . have not
yet entered into the world."[25] The important difference is that
now instead of being contained by it, consciousness contains it.
It is "Noon—without the News of Night," because now nothing
remains alienated from consciousness. This rendezvous of light
appears frequently when a threshold is crossed from a world of
limits and temporality to one of union accompanied by complete
consciousness, as we have seen in 1053 and as we see in the
following poem:

At last, to be identified!
At last, the lamps upon thy side
The rest of Life to *see*!

Past Midnight! Past the Morning Star!
Past Sunrise!
Ah, What leagues there *were*
Between our feet, and Day!   [174]

The past tense of the verb in the last stanza is emphasized to
show the difference between the "day" she thought was such and

the pure, absolute Day that ends this poem and "To my small Hearth." The more specific image in the latter of a permanent noon is one she frequently uses: "'Heaven' has different Signs— to me— / Sometimes, I think that Noon / Is but a symbol of the Place" (575). Perhaps the most effective and explicit use of the symbol for a world of extended consciousness is:

> There is a Zone whose even Years
> No Solstice interrupt—
> Whose Sun constructs perpetual Noon
> Whose perfect Seasons wait—
>
> Whose Summer set in Summer, till
> The Centuries of June
> And Centuries of August cease
> And Consciousness—is Noon. [1056]

This is a zone beyond limits and demarcations; there are no sol-stices here, just as in "Wild Nights" there is no need for compass and chart. Because noon is "Degreeless" (287)—the hands of the clock align perfectly; the sundial shows a thin line, not a broad shadow—it is the perfect temporal image to represent that which is beyond time. Dickinson's symbols for what Jung would call the individuated psyche are similar to Emerson's vision of the humble-bee as a "voyager of light and noon" (9:40).

The poems of Emily Dickinson, then, create an equivalence between love and death—an equivalence that is not arbitrary or fanciful but rooted in the realities of psychic experience. In another article, Rosemary Gordon writes about several of her patients who are overtly afraid of death, but for whom also "the relationship to death really has something of a teasing, a flirting quality."[26] David McClelland also writes of encountering often "a person, usually a woman, who not only does not fear death but actually appears to be looking forward to it with a sense of excite-ment. The possibility both thrills and attracts her, at the same time that it frightens her. Yet often the thrill seems as strong as the fear, in much the same way that it is for a person who is about

to make a ski jump or a very high dive."[27] These observations are
given some empirical support by Ellen Greenberger in her study
"Fantasies of Women Confronting Death."[28] Greenberger tested
two groups of women—one consisting of hospital patients who
knew they were terminally ill, and the other a control group of
women in the same hospitals for very minor operations. The main
instrument was the Thematic Apperception Test, in which the
subject is asked to make up stories about an ambiguous series of
pictures. Greenberger discovered that those women for whom
death was an immediate possibility thought about sex almost
twice as often as those in the control group. Moreover, there was
"an increase in themes of illicit sexuality. The specific imagery included in this category dealt with rape, abduction, seduction, and
infidelity. Curiously, these episodes involved a man whose identity was very nebulous. In considering the identity of the male,
it was suggested that perhaps Death itself was the mysterious
lover."[29]
Dickinson, as far as we know, was unaware of a specific terminal disease, but as a poet and as one whose life was fairly bare
of external circumstance, she was more in touch than most of us
with the basic human situation, with the sentence of death we are
all under. In one poem she writes:

I read my sentence—steadily—
Reviewed it with my eyes,
To see that I made no mistake
In it's extremest clause—
The Date, and manner, of the shame—
And then the Pious Form
That "God have mercy" on the Soul
The Jury voted Him—
I made my soul familiar—with her extremity—
That at the last, it should not be a novel Agony—
But she, and Death, acquainted—
Meet tranquilly, as friends—
Salute, and pass, without a Hint—
And there, the Matter ends—   [412]

The incipient pun, along with its incipient hope, in the last line, where perhaps this is the end only of "the Matter," the body, is undercut by the earlier notion of God having mercy on the soul as a "Pious Form." The "extremest clause" of the "sentence" is also the "extremity" of the "soul"—period.

The similarities in imagery and tone between the stories told by the women facing death and the poems of Dickinson are often startling. For example, the following, told about a picture of a couple embracing, maintains the same tension among love, death, and spirituality that we have noted in Dickinson poems: "I first thought it looks like he's enticing her, if he's a he, but I don't like the theme of enticement. He's imparting some kind of message— a very special message. It has such an ethereal quality. He's telling—assuring her, that something is all right, but I'll be damned if I know what. What could it be? It looks like a romantic theme, but I'm trying to steer away from a romantic theme."[30] It is difficult to view, however, the set of complexes and dynamics involved as specifically or predominantly "feminine," as Gordon and McClelland imply, especially because Greenberger's study did not also include groups of men for comparative purposes and because we have seen complementary images and attitudes in the work of Poe. And yet a juxtaposition of the poems with what has remained of the myths of our less patriarchal past yields fruitful congruences. Of particular relevance is the series of myths grouped by two Jungian scholars, Joseph Henderson and Maud Oakes,[31] in which a woman descends or is taken off to the world of the dead only to experience rebirth and transformation.

The most important version of this myth in our Western culture is that of Persephone, which has been preserved in its earliest written form in the *Homeric Hymn to Demeter*. According to the *Hymn*, the maiden Persephone was gathering flowers in a lush meadow with her friends, the daughters of Oceanus. As she picked crocuses, roses, and violets, she saw a narcissus

> which Earth, as a trick, grew for this girl, as a favor for
> Him Who Receives So Many and with Zeus allowing it (its
> brightness was wonderful!). It astonished everyone who saw

it, immortal gods and mortal men alike. From its root it
pushed up a hundred heads and a fragrance from its top
making all the vast sky above smile, and all the earth and
all the salt swelling of the sea. And she was astonished too,
she stretched out both her hands to pick this delightful thing.
But the earth, wide with roads, opened up! in the Nysian
Plain, and out came He Who Receives So Many, with his
immortal horses, that son of Cronos with so many names.
And he grabbed her, resisting, and he took her in his gold
chariot, weeping.[32]

Persephone's mother, Demeter, goddess of the harvest, was struck
with grief and anger, and did not let the earth grow plants. Zeus
interceded with his brother Hades, so that the latter agreed to let
Persephone return to her mother. But before Hades drove her
back up to the earth's surface, he gave her a pomegranate seed.
Mother and daughter then had a blissful reunion, but afterwards
Demeter told Persephone that because she had eaten the seed in
the Underworld, she must live a third of each year there as Hades'
wife. "For the other two parts," said Demeter, "you will live with
me and the other gods. And whenever the earth blossoms with all
kinds of fragrant Spring flowers, you will come back up again
from the mist darkness."[33]

In investigating the meanings of the *Hymn*, we must remember
that characters in myth are not portrayed with a high degree
of psychological complexity. Although Persephone screams and
weeps while being abducted, there are reasons to believe that she
is not entirely repelled either by Hades or by life in the Underworld. Instead of this attraction emerging as part of a psychological ambivalence, it is displaced on the enticing narcissus.
The connection of the flower with death itself is supported by
etymology: narcissus is so named for its narcotic properties (*narké*
means numbness or stupor). Indeed, more time is spent in the
Hymn on the attractiveness of the flower than on the terror of the
sudden abduction.

In Dickinson's poetry, on the other hand, ambivalences like this
are expressed by the very movement of the verse in the mind of a

single speaker. We can juxtapose the opening of the *Hymn* with a Dickinson poem, not necessarily to make a case for direct influence, but to show how they can mutually illuminate each other and the psyche. We should not, however, rule out the myth as a source, especially because the September 1859 issue of the *Atlantic Monthly* contained an interpretation of "The Eleusinia," the rites most closely connected with the *Hymn*: "Not to Demeter, then, nor even to Isis, do the Eleusinia primarily point, but to the human heart. We no longer look at them; henceforth they are within us."[34]

> Of Death I try to think like this—
> The Well in which they lay us
> Is but the Likeness of the Brook
> That menaced not to slay us,
> But to invite by that Dismay
> Which is the Zest of sweetness
> To the same Flower Hesperian,
> Decoying but to greet us—
>
> I do remember when a Child
> With bolder Playmates straying
> To where a Brook that seemed a Sea
> Withheld us by it's roaring
> From just a Purple Flower beyond
> Until constrained to clutch it
> If Doom itself were the result,
> The boldest leaped, and clutched it—   [1558]

In the poem, confusion and ambivalence about death are rendered in the structure and syntax; reading the poem becomes an experience of "that Dismay / Which is the Zest of sweetness." For example, it is difficult to make sense of the first stanza until after we have read the second, which gives us a specific scene depicting the spatial relationships among brook, flower, and children. Similarly, the second stanza is a long, periodic, hypotactic sentence, comprehensible only after we read it in its entirety and sort it out. This kind of motion makes the reading of the poem a headlong rush that ends not in resolution, but in suspension. As in some other Dickinson poems, the closing dashes suggest not so much termination as interruption or omission.[35] Is Doom the result? And, in a question like one raised in the suitor poems, is the flower the beautiful thing it appears or a deceptive, ominous lure like the narcissus? Should the fourth line be read as the brook threatening the children so that they will not be killed, or as the brook not threatening the children in order to seduce them into taking the risk? Should not the flower (or the brook?) be greeting the children in order to decoy them, rather than—as line eight suggests—the other way around?

No clear answers emerge from the poem itself, only a compounding of these complexities, as we see in the double-edged quality of the adjectives that modify "Flower" in each of the stanzas. "Hesperian" in Dickinson's Lexicon is defined as "Western," presumably after the Greek myth of the Hesperides, the Isles of the Blessed beyond the river-ocean at the extreme western limits of the world, the land of the carefully guarded golden apples. The word is also given resonance by Hesperus, the evening star that shines brightly just after the sun has set. Does the word suggest a golden paradise or a perilous journey to destruction? Do the natural cycles of the sun and the star indicate renewal also in the human sphere, or are they just metaphoric fables when applied to our fate? Similarly, "Purple" is a color both of royalty and mourning, and is used in this dual role in several poems, most famously: "One dignity delays for all— / One mitred Afternoon— / None can avoid this purple— / None evade this Crown!" (98).

More central and more complex than the flower imagery, though, is the water imagery. First, the grave is metaphorically turned into a well and the well likened to a brook, and then in the second stanza the brook seems a sea—a rather sudden increase in scope, power, and turbulence that parallels the movement both in "To my small Hearth" and in the *Hymn*, where a playful outing turns into an adventure of cosmic proportions and implications. The "Sea" here is related to the sea we first encountered in "Wild Nights"—a vast, boundless realm whose inner counterpart is the self. Dickinson writes in a letter to a friend: "The shore is safer,

Abiah, but I love to buffet the sea—I can count the bitter wrecks here in these pleasant waters, and hear the murmuring winds, but oh, I love the danger!"[36] Whatever else is unclear or ambivalent about this poem, there is definitely here too a sense of excitement, an exultation, that the speaker not only does feel but—as the first line tells us—tries to and wants to feel about death. As in Rolfe Humphries's revision of Hotspur's line, "Out of this nettle, safety, we pluck this flower, danger." As Dickinson writes in the first line of another poem: " 'Tis so appalling—it exhilarates" (281). And in another poem she uses the same word "dismay" to describe the approach-avoidance conflict generated by "Old Suitor Heaven":

> We shun it ere it comes,
> Afraid of Joy,
> Then sue it to delay
> And lest it fly,
> Beguile it more and more—
> May not this be
> Old Suitor Heaven
> Like our dismay at thee?   [1580]

Just as we earlier looked at three poems about death as a suitor that have the same mythic suggestiveness and reflect the same psychological complexes as the abduction of Persephone by Hades, so we can isolate a set of three other poems to serve as the marriage group, paralleling the wedding-night consummation of Death and the maiden. We notice immediately the suddenness and the thoroughness of the transformation, and the inseparableness of the spiritual and the sexual.

> I'm "wife"—I've finished that—
> That other state—
> I'm Czar—I'm "Woman" now—
> It's safer so—
>
> How odd the Girl's life looks
> Behind this soft Eclipse—

I think that Earth feels so
To folks in Heaven—now—

This being comfort—then
That other kind—was pain—
But why compare?
I'm "Wife"! Stop there!   [199]

A Wife—at Daybreak I shall be—
Sunrise—Hast thou a Flag for me?
At Midnight, I am but a Maid,
How short it takes to make it Bride—
Then—Midnight, I have passed from thee
Unto the East, and Victory—

Midnight—Good Night! I hear them call,
The Angels bustle in the Hall—
Softly my Future climbs the Stair,
I fumble at my Childhood's prayer
So soon to be a Child no more—
Eternity, I'm coming—Sir,
Savior—I've seen the face—before!   [461]

I'm ceded—I've stopped being Their's—
The name They dropped upon my face
With water, in the country church
Is finished using, now,
And They can put it with my Dolls,
My childhood, and the string of spools,
I've finished threading—too—

Baptized, before, without the choice,
But this time, consciously, of Grace—
Unto supremest name—
Called to my Full—The Crescent dropped—
Existence's whole Arc, filled up,
With one small Diadem.

My second Rank—too small the first—
Crowned—Crowing—on my Father's breast—

A half unconscious Queen—
But this time—Adequate—Erect,
With Will to choose, or to reject,
And I choose, just a Crown—   [508]

As Albert Gelpi writes of the first stanza of the first poem: "The passage from virgin to wife is not a matter of maidenhead but of psychological depths. And the activation of inert potentialities, the summoning of the unconscious to consciousness, make the poet realize herself simultaneously, almost equally as masculine and feminine: 'I'm Czar—I'm "Woman" now—.' Becoming Czar is not the opposite of becoming Woman. One's incompleteness becomes whole by finding the 'other' in one's self."[37] The synesthetic symbol of the "soft Eclipse" in the next stanza is particularly appropriate for depicting this movement of expansiveness: light or darkness is completely a matter of perspective and position, and psychic occlusions can affect only those away from the center of full consciousness. The movement from partial to full consciousness is also rendered in the next poem through darkness/light contrasts, but the natural cycle of midnight and sunrise suggests not so much opposition as complementarity and development. The speaker is bidding farewell to Midnight, but also calling it "Good Night," and the imagery in the next two lines suggests Jacob's prophetic dream of fulfillment. The imagery in the third poem, though, is perhaps the most effective and suggestive: "Called to my Full—the Crescent dropped— / Existence's whole Arc filled up, / With one small Diadem." The entire sphere of the moon exists—although mainly in uroboric darkness—even when only a small sliver of it is lit. Yet as naturally and as inexorably as day follows night will the entire circle be illuminated ("the rest of Life to *see!*"). In all three poems, but especially in the last, the child/adult distinction is superimposed on the maiden/wife one, linking the darkness/light imagery more closely with 1 Corinthians 13:11–12: "When I was child, I spake as a child, I understood as a child, I thought as a child: but when I became a man I put away childish things. For now we see through a glass, darkly; but then face to face: now I know in part; but then shall I know even as I am known."

A surprising addition, however, is the last line of the second poem, "Savior—I've seen the face—before!" This is the kind of line that demonstrates the interrelated levels on which much of the best poetry works, for it generates a series of meanings that do not exclude but enrich each other. On one level, the speaker has seen the face of the savior through her acute sensitivity to the wonders of the everyday, to what Whitman calls "the dazzle of the light and of every moment of your life" (84). Emily Dickinson writes: "The Only News I know / Is Bulletins all Day / From Immortality" (827). At another level, she has seen the savior's face in the faces of those she has loved on earth, in ways suggested by the Yeats quotation given earlier and by her own lines: "Not Either—noticed Death— / Of Paradise—aware— / Each other's Face—was all the Disc / Each other's setting—saw—" (474). And at perhaps the most general and deepest level are those direct intimations of individuation that we have had precisely because we were children, once completely in a state of paradisal unity. This implication is clearest in the last of the three poems, where the speaker talks about two states of grace, one before she put away childish things and the other in full consciousness and free choice. The sense of dependence, merger, even engulfment suggested by "Crowned—Crowing—on my Father's breast— / A half unconscious Queen" gives way to a situation in which male and female, now completely differentiated can rejoin in a union as equal sexual partners, not as parent and child or God and human.

The choice of these three poems to represent the marriage consummation stresses the expansion of consciousness through the *hieros gamos*, as opposed to those poems that extend the more sinister possibilities of the death as suitor motif, where darkness and silence reign, such as:

What Inn is this
Where for the night
Peculiar Traveller comes?

Who is the Landlord?
Where the maids?
Behold, what curious rooms!
No ruddy fires on the hearth—
No brimming Tankards flow—
Necromancer! Landlord!
Who are these below?   [115]

This emphasis may seem out of keeping with the myth itself,
where Persephone is taken from a realm of light and pleasure to
one of darkness and death, but it is actually closer to the deeper
meanings of the myth and the rituals associated with it. For the
necessary complement of Persephone's abduction and descent into
the Underworld is her return to the earth's surface, involving her
fusion with the natural cycles of fertility. The double movement
represents essentially an experience of rebirth and transformation, where the end becomes a new beginning.

To draw some of these connections more closely, we can examine
the following poem:

A solemn thing—it was—I said—
A Woman—white—to be—
And wear—if God should count me fit—
Her blameless mystery—

A timid thing—to drop a life
Into the mystic well—
Too plummetless—that it come back—
Eternity—until—

I pondered how the bliss would look—
And would it feel as big—
When I could take it in my hand—
As hovering—seen—through fog—

And then—the size of this "small" life—
The Sages—call it small—
Swelled—like Horizons—in my breast—
And I sneered—softly—"small"!   [271]

The poem is a good example of how basic opposites are related and contained. In the first stanza, for example, the poet gives us a double perspective on the wearing of white: on the one hand it stands for sexual innocence, but on the other, it is worn by a "Woman" who is about to enter or has entered the kind of marriage we have already seen described. Virginity can thus be viewed as primarily the readiness, the ripeness for consummation. A similar double meaning has already been discussed in connection with the word "purple," which is a variant for "mystic" in the second stanza, and here we again encounter the image of a well for a grave. The well may seem to be the plummetless avenue to oblivion, but it is also the unfathomable source of life. Dickinson writes in other poems: "Let Brooks—renew of Brooks— / But Wells—of failless Ground!" (1091) and "What mystery pervades a well! / . . . Like looking every time you please / In an abyss's face!" (1400). The speaker's "small" life swelling like horizons in her breast epitomizes the movement we have seen in "To my small Hearth" and "Of Death I try to think like this," and suggests a basic sexual dimension in this experience of expanded being.

The central paradox of the poem is the one celebrated in the myth of Persephone and the rites at Eleusis: that to drop the individual life into the well of death actually ushers one into a larger sphere of life beyond personal existence. Once one moves beyond the limits of the ego, one can see that the vast territory beyond it is also life. As McClelland writes, the Eleusinian mysteries celebrated the nearly universal idea that one must "surrender or go down in order to come up, give of oneself in order to get, *die to live*."[38] This paradox is further embodied in the harvest and seed symbolism in both the rites and the poems. In the ancient Greek ceremonies, as in similar ones that have come down from basically neolithic farming cultures, the reaping of the harvest was ritually associated with the planting of next year's seed, death intimately related to rebirth. Pindar comments: "Blessed is he who having seen these rites, goes below the hollow earth; for he knows the end of life and he knows its god-sent beginning."[39] Also commenting specifically on the rites associ-

ated with the Persephone myth, Jung writes of a typical partici-
pant: "The conscious experience of these ties produces the feeling
that her life is spread over generations—the first step towards
the immediate experience and conviction of being outside time,
which brings with it a feeling of *immortality*."[40]
These images and psychological dynamics find expression in
Dickinson's poems, such as:

Midsummer, was it, when They died—
A full, and perfect time—
The Summer closed upon itself
In Consummated Bloom—

The Corn, her furthest kernel filled
Before the coming Flail—
When These—leaned into Perfectness—
Through Haze of Burial—   [962]

The summer solstice is the Noon of the year, and as such is a time
that points beyond time; the summer here closes upon itself as in
"There is a Zone," where the centuries of June and August cease.
The second stanza suggests that the "Consummated Bloom" will
become by that very fact "the perennial bloom" mentioned in
another poem (195). The haze of burial here is like the fog in the
last poem, the obscurities and mysteries that surround death, but
through which the realization of continued life finally pierces.

The image in "Midsummer, was it," of the circle completed turn-
ing into a new dimension of being, with its suggestions of both the
natural cycles and the psychic return to its primordial unity,
brings us back to the most famous of Dickinson's poems, "Because
I could not stop for Death." In the third stanza of that poem,
particularly, is the sense of completing a full and perfect circle.
As the carriage embarks on its spatial movement towards the
cemetery, we get a compressed vision of the temporal movement
toward the grave—childhood, where the figures are arranged in a
"Ring"; the ripening of maturity, in the fields of grain; and dying,
in the setting sun. Significantly, these three stages are repre-

sented by images from what we usually think of as three separate realms: the human, the organic but nonhuman, and the larger movement of the cosmos. The focal point is shifted at the beginning of the next stanza: "Or rather—He passed Us," suggesting the Copernican revolution in the psyche mentioned earlier. This, together with the interrelations among the three realms, makes us more receptive to the archetypal connections underlying the ancient rites and forming also a deep substratum of the Christian myth. We are prepared now to view "A Swelling of the Ground" as the promise of life instead of its denial. As in "A solemn thing," "Swelling" unites human sexuality—both male tumescence and its frequent result in the female, pregnancy—with the fertility of crops, the growing and swelling seed, the shoots pushing out from the earth. Both are linked to the psychic or spiritual expansion that consciousness of the processes creates. A crux in this stanza is the use of the identical rhyme on "Ground," a device that is rarely seen in Dickinson, and that strikes the ear a little oddly here. But this device underscores a paronomastic reading of the fourth line as "The Corn is in the Ground," with its world of meaning epitomized in John 12:24–25: "Verily, verily, I say unto you, Except a corn of wheat fall into the ground and die, it abideth alone: but if it die, it bringeth forth much fruit. He that loveth his life shall lose it; and he that hateth his life in this world shall keep it unto life eternal."

We can see here, and in other poems we have looked at, the convergence of the ancient Eleusinian rites with Christian themes and imagery, similar to the more historical and analytic connections made by anthropologists and students of comparative religion. In the *Atlantic* article on Eleusis that Dickinson almost surely read, we find: "Thus is recognized the intimate connection which our lady has with the movements of Nature, in which her life is mirrored—especially with the rising, the ongoing, and the waning of the day. . . . But prominently, as in all worship, are our eyes turned toward the East,—toward the resurrection."[41] Dickinson asks, "Sunrise—Hast thou a Flag for me?" (461). This is not to argue, however, that the meanings of Dickinson's poetry are ultimately or merely "Christian." Rather than accepting and using Christian symbols as given cultural forms, she refashions them through her inner experience and by this process manages to reinvest them with some of their most powerful symbolic resonances. She uncovers what Emerson would call the "fossil poetry" (3:22) of the Christian myth, giving us a personal and emotional etymology of it.

This is clear in the Indian Summer poems, where the imagery of Eleusis is fused with the Christian symbolism that in some ways superseded it.

> These are the days when Birds come back—
> A very few—a Bird or two—
> To take a backward look.
>
> These are the days when skies resume
> The old—old sophistries of June—
> A blue and gold mistake.
>
> Oh fraud that cannot cheat the Bee—
> Almost thy plausibility
> Induces my belief.
>
> Till ranks of seed their witness bear—
> And softly thro' the altered air
> Hurries a timid leaf.
>
> Oh Sacrament of summer days,
> Oh Last Communion in the Haze—
> Permit a child to join.
>
> Thy sacred emblems to partake—
> Thy consecrated bread to take
> And thine immortal wine!   [130]

Clark Griffith maintains that Indian Summer in this poem is a cruel hoax: "For, in the main, it seems the business of temporality and mutability to undermine the foundations of human faith."[42] But in the light of what we have seen, the poem has exactly the

opposite meaning—temporality and mutability are the foundations of faith to those who know the secrets of Eleusis. There is
always change, but the change is always patterned. The bee is not
"cheated" because it is a creature of the moment, unaware of
what the human mind, which can move through time, knows
about the cycles of death and rebirth. Through further observation and meditation the fraud becomes not only plausible but
certain; Indian Summer is not itself Spring, but the very presence
of new life in the midst of decline makes it an augury or a symbol
of Spring. The Christian imagery is not being undercut or sati-
rized as much as it is being reattached to visible and natural
things, instead of remaining abstract and conventional signs. The
tone in the last two stanzas is particularly exultant, assured. It
is the same voice that in another Indian Summer poem can say
of the departing leaves: "Departing then—forever— / Forever—
until May— / Forever is deciduous—" (1422).

In Emily Dickinson's poetry, then, the images of death, sacred
marriage, and rebirth become the basic symbolic enactments in
the drama of a mind moving toward individuation. The movement
is neither linear nor direct, but the poems can be arranged to
correspond to what is both a basic ritual pattern and the sequence
of psychic development. As Henderson writes: "'Separation' is
followed by 'transition' which is followed by 'incorporation.' This
is experienced no longer in the outer ceremonial of past times,
but inwardly as a meaningful procession of images: from descent
to a death as sacrifice, there is passage to a sacred marriage
rite, thence to a symbol of new birth from this union and an
ascent and re-emergence into a light of that consciousness which
has the power to redeem and reunite those elements of ego or of
Self which were originally unconscious."[43] With typical compression and power, Dickinson charts symbolically this journey from
limited awareness to a center of consciousness that radiates out
into the entire psychic realm.

The inundation of the Spring
Enlarges every soul—

It sweeps the tenement away
But leaves the Water whole—

In which the soul at first estranged—
Seeks faintly for it's shore
But acclimated—pines no more
For that Peninsula—   [1425]

AFTERWORD

American Romanticism can be viewed as part of the progressive self-discovery of the psyche. The Delphic injunction to know oneself becomes a radical and immediate venture in a land perceived as the embodiment of the unknown. When Whitman correlated outward and westward exploration with psychic expansion in poems such as "Passage to India," he was elaborating on an already pervasive *topos* in American literature. In the Reality segment of "Experience," Emerson writes: "I am ready to die out of nature and be born again into this new yet unapproachable America I have found in the West" (3:72). Thoreau asks, "What does the West stand for? Is not our own interior white on the chart?" An exploring expedition is "but an indirect recognition of the fact, that there are continents and seas in the moral world, to which every man is an isthmus or an inlet, yet unexplored by him."[1] Dickinson, as often, is the most concise:

> Soto! Explore Thyself!
> Therein thyself shalt find
> The "Undiscovered Continent"—
> No Settler had the Mind.   [832]

With typical Dickinson word play, the last line also suggests that
nothing and no one can permanently "settle" or satisfy the mind,
never: the quest is perpetual.

This study has not so much sought to settle as to lure others
further and deeper into unexplored spaces. As is evident from
its length, it has sought to be suggestive rather than comprehensive, exemplifying rather than exhausting its method and subject
matter. It has adopted precisely the opposite strategy of Marie
Bonaparte's mammoth psychoanalytic study of Poe, where similar
tales are individually given similar analyses always leading to
the same conclusions: "For the very monotony of these tales, their
endless repetition, are themselves expressions of Poe's psyche."[2]
This is the critical equivalent of the imitative fallacy in art. I
would argue, rather, that a critical hypothesis should not have to
cover any and all applications; literary criticism should be subject to criteria analogous to replicability in the sciences. If other
critics and scholars cannot make use—in however modified and
refined forms—of the ideas and approaches here, these may not
have much validity in the first place, and no further proliferation
of my own examples is likely to change the situation.

The brevity of the study, however, may raise the suspicion that
particular authors or texts were chosen for the particular metaphoric congruities I am trying to establish and exploit. It would
contradict my pluralistic and pragmatic bias either to deny this
accusation completely or to see it as a grave methodological error.
The most sensitive and careful Jungian readings, for example,
of such Hawthorne tales as "Roger Malvin's Burial" or "Alice
Doane's Appeal" would probably not meet with the successes
Frederick Crews has achieved from his Freudian standpoint.[3]
Conversely, Stephen Black's readings of Whitman's unitary and
expansive visions as regressions to infantile narcissism tell us
little either about the texts or about the possibilities open for
consciousness.[4] But to allay this suspicion more directly, I must
say that in the actual writing of the book, the opposite was more
of a problem: at a certain point the framework seemed to apply
almost every place I looked. I took this as a signal to step back, to
consolidate and focus, rather than to pursue the many apparently

promising directions. I felt that in this case I could save the rest for another day, if that seemed appropriate, if with more distance I were still sure I was not mistaking the map for the territory itself.

For previous literary criticism, using a Jungian base has often rightly met with resistance because it claimed too much for itself; it gave its maps more adherence and credence than maps of such unsurveyed regions merit, sometimes prematurely sketching in the interior white. It saw itself uncovering universal and eternal archetypes without allowing for the culture-bound and historically shaped components of Jung's own system. Such a recognition does limit and qualify the application of Jungian thought, but it can also clarify and center it on those areas where it is most appropriate. This study has argued its value and appropriateness as a hermeneutics for works written in hermetic, illuminist, and Romantic traditions. I am personally skeptical of its continuing usefulness as a clinical psychology until more systematic and empirical studies are made, and the results of those studies incorporated into its theory and practice. I also have to plead agnosticism about the actual existence of the collective unconscious and its archetypes, not only because the jury is still out on such fundamental questions as the nature of the mind, but because of the epistemological status of these concepts. As Jung points out, the archetypes by their very nature can never be known directly, but "only from the effects they produce,"[5] from their symbols or other manifestations. Any evidence of the collective unconscious must necessarily be conscious, and therefore no longer the thing *an sich*. This is not to deflate such concepts, but to stress their nature as hypotheses that are very difficult either to prove or to disprove. As literary critics, however, we can appropriate them as sometimes illuminating analogies and take the system as a convenient, self-explicating symbology. As we look at American Romanticism, we see that Jungian thought gives perspective and coherence to what at closer range may seem eccentrically individual visions, and often provides the most appropriate metaphors for our metaphors, nearly supreme fictions for the fictions that engage us most deeply.

NOTES

I. Mythodology: The Symbol in Jungian Thought and American Romanticism

1. Although Frederick Crews does not make this argument, he presents an intelligent case in *Out of My System*, pp. 166–85, for the value of a reductive critical thesis when used flexibly and creatively. Crews maintains that "to be a critic is precisely to take a stance different from the author's and to pursue a thesis of one's own," p. 184. This is a valid and often productive critical position, which the present study does not seek to refute but to go beyond.

2. Northrop Frye, *Spiritus Mundi*, p. 102.

3. As quoted in Jolande Jacobi, *Complex/Archetype/Symbol in the Psychology of C. G. Jung*, p. 118. This translation is by Ralph Manheim; the corresponding passage in C. G. Jung, *Collected Works*, ed. Herbert Read, Michael Fordham, Gerhard Adler, and William McGuire, trans. R. F. C. Hull, 2d ed., 18 vols. (Princeton: Princeton University Press, 1967–79, Bollingen Series XX), is on p. 253 of vol. 6, *Psychological Types*. Further works by Jung cited with a volume number preceding the title are from this edition of the *Collected Works*.

4. James A. Coulter, *The Literary Microcosm*, p. 61. The phrases within double quotation marks are from Liddell and Scott, *Greek-English Lexicon*, new ed.

5. Leopold Stein, "What Is a Symbol Supposed to Be?" p. 75. See also Rosemary Gordon, "Symbols," pp. 293–304, and Jacobi, *Complex/Archetype/Symbol*, pp. 74–124.

6. Jung, vol. 6: *Psychological Types*, p. 474. The emphasis here is from the original source, as are all other emphases in quotations from Jung.

7. Ralph Waldo Emerson, *The Complete Works of Ralph Waldo Emerson*, ed. Edward Waldo Emerson, Centenary Edition, 12 vols. (Boston and New York: Houghton Mifflin, 1903–4), 2:308. All quotations from this edition are indicated, as here, by parentheses within the text citing volume and page numbers. Words emphasized the first time a passage is quoted are always those emphasized in this source.

8. As quoted in Jacobi, *Complex/Archetype/Symbol*, pp. 98–99. The corresponding passage can be found in Jung, vol. 13: *Alchemical Studies*, p. 163.

9. See Jung, vol. 11: *Psychology and Religion*, p. 275.

10. Jung, vol. 15: *The Spirit in Man, Art, and Literature*, pp. 75–76.

11. Jeffrey L. Duncan, *The Power and Form of Emerson's Thought*, p. 4.

12. Jung, vol. 14: *Mysterium Coniunctionis*, p. 180.

13. Erich Neumann, *The Origins and History of Consciousness*, pp. 7, 8.

14. Horace Bushnell, "Preliminary Dissertation on the Nature of Language, as Related to Thought and Spirit," pp. 93, 96.

15. Walt Whitman, *Leaves of Grass*, ed. Harold W. Blodgett and Sculley Bradley, Comprehensive Reader's Edition (New York: New York University Press, 1965), p. 8. All quotations from this edition are indicated, as here, by parentheses within the text citing page number or numbers. Words emphasized the first time a passage is quoted are always those emphasized in this source.

16. Emily Dickinson, *The Poems of Emily Dickinson, Including Variant Readings Critically Compared with All Known Manuscripts*, ed. Thomas H. Johnson, 3 vols. (Cambridge: Harvard University Press, 1955), poem number 1129. All quotations from the poetry are from this edition and are indicated, as here, by parentheses within the text giving the number of the poem. The versions in this study are the first ones as they appear in the Johnson text.

17. Jung, vol. 7: *Two Essays on Analytical Psychology*, p. 291.

18. To see that this method by itself is no assurance of success or failure, we can compare two recent critical applications. Edward F. Edinger's *Melville's Moby-Dick* wanders needlessly far from the text

without realizing the ways in which the novel amplifies and interprets itself. In *The Roots of Horror in the Fiction of H. P. Lovecraft*, on the other hand, Barton Levi St. Armand fruitfully juxtaposes a short story by the horror writer with a dream of Jung to bring out obscured resonances and meanings in both. Two other effective applications of amplification to myths and literature are Erich Neumann, *Amor and Psyche*, and Heinrich Zimmer, *The King and the Corpse*.

19. This list is not an attempt to establish a Great Tradition in the criticism of American literature, but it does focus on those books that attempt major syntheses of movements or periods rather than concentrating on a single author or on a more narrow perspective.

20. Although these articles are concerned with a single author, a piece such as "Usher Unveiled," pp. 1–8, makes accessible to the critic formerly unsuspected sources and approaches to American texts.

21. There is some risk of oversimplification in designating such an approach, but it is the strategy followed by Bruce Kuklick in "Myth and Symbol in American Studies," p. 435 n, where he cites the authority of Leo Marx's "American Studies—A Defense of an Unscientific Method," pp. 75–76, for grouping together the specific authors and books. The title of Michael J. Colacurcio's review essay, "The Symbolic and the Symptomatic: D. H. Lawrence in Recent American Criticism," suggests even more wide-sweeping and tenuous connections.

22. Charles Feidelson, Jr., *Symbolism and American Literature*, p. 5. Emerson's centrality and influence receive even greater emphasis in Hyatt H. Waggoner, *American Poets from the Puritans to the Present*, and more recently in David Porter, *Emerson and Literary Change*. See R. A. Yoder, *Emerson and the Orphic Poet in America*, pp. 207–8, for a brief but helpful guide to current critical interest in Emerson. Although the present study acknowledges Emerson's centrality, it does not take this as the single explanatory or determining factor; that the kinds of configurations this book traces can often be seen equally well in a contemporary but in some ways antithetical figure like Poe suggests patterns of thought and feeling that go beyond any single writer.

23. The relevant titles and ideas of Frye and Abrams are presented in Chapter 3, but it is appropriate to mention here, near the related issue of Emerson's centrality, Harold Bloom's *Figures of Capable Imagination*, pp. 46–233, which views our most important modern and contemporary poets as sharing in Romantic and visionary traditions, as evidenced in assertions such as the following: "Romanticism, even in its most remorseless protagonists, is centrally a humanism, which seeks our renewal as

makers, which hopes to give us the immodest hope that we—even we—coming so late in time's injustices can still sing a song of ourselves" (p. 57).

24. Feidelson, *Symbolism and American Literature*, p. 4.

25. Kuklick, "Myth and Symbol," p. 441.

26. Colacurcio, "The Symbolic and the Symptomatic," p. 494. The specific work of E. D. Hirsch referred to is *Validity in Interpretation.*

27. Colacurcio, "The Symbolic and the Symptomatic," p. 495.

28. Nathaniel Hawthorne, *Mosses from an Old Manse*, pp. 74, 76, 84.

29. Robert D. Richardson, Jr., *Myth and Literature in the American Renaissance*, p. 5.

30. Richardson is one of our foremost experts in the historical development of mythography, as evinced in the impressive compilation, with extensive commentary, *The Rise of Modern Mythology, 1680–1860*, by Burton Feldman and Robert D. Richardson, Jr.

31. Heinrich Zimmer, *Myths and Symbols in Indian Art and Civilization*, p. 221.

II. Voyages of the Mind's Return: Three Paradigmatic Works

1. See especially M. H. Abrams, *Natural Supernaturalism*, and Northrop Frye, *A Study of English Romanticism.*

2. Edgar Allan Poe, *The Complete Works of Edgar Allan Poe*, ed. James A. Harrison, 17 vols. (1902; reprint ed., New York: AMS Press, 1965). All prose quotations from Poe are from this edition and are indicated, as here, by parentheses within the text citing volume and page numbers. The generous use of emphases in these quotations is entirely Poe's own.

3. For the most valuable of these studies see Maurice Beebe, "The Universe of Roderick Usher," pp. 147–60; John F. Lynen, *The Design of the Present*, pp. 205–71; and Eric W. Carlson, *Poe on the Soul of Man.*

4. Compare, for example, *Marginalia* (16:10) with *Eureka* (16:292).

5. Daniel Hoffman, *Poe Poe Poe Poe Poe Poe Poe*, pp. 278–80. See also H. Bruce Franklin, *Future Perfect*, pp. 99–102.

6. Erich Neumann, *The Great Mother*, p. 19 n.

7. Alan C. Golding, "Reductive and Expansive Language," p. 5.

8. Ralph Waldo Emerson, *The Journals and Miscellaneous Notebooks of Ralph Waldo Emerson*, ed. William H. Gilman et al., 14 vols. (Cam-

bridge: Harvard University Press, 1960–78), 9:332–33. All further references to Emerson's journals are to this edition, abbreviated *JMN*.

9. Friedrich Creuzer, *Symbolism and Mythology of Ancient Peoples*, from the selection and translation in Feldman and Richardson, *The Rise of Modern Mythology*, pp. 391–92. For Creuzer's influence on Emerson and other transcendentalists, see Richardson, *Myth and Literature*, p. 49.

10. Feldman and Richardson, *The Rise of Modern Mythology*, p. 392.

11. Howard J. Waskow, *Whitman*, p. 157.

12. Walt Whitman, *Prose Works, 1892*, 1:259.

13. See particularly two early studies, Frederic I. Carpenter, *Emerson and Asia*, and Arthur E. Christy, *The Orient in American Transcendentalism*. For a more theoretical discussion, see James Baird, *Ishmael*.

14. Henry D. Thoreau, *A Week on the Concord and Merrimack Rivers*, p. 150.

15. Herman Melville, *Mardi, and a Voyage Thither*, p. 551.

16. Emerson, *JMN*, 11:201.

17. Nathaniel Hawthorne, *The House of the Seven Gables*, p. 259.

III. One's Self I Sing: Individuation and Introjection

1. See, for example, E. A. Bennet, *C. G. Jung*, p. 138, and Edward F. Edinger, *Ego and Archetype*, p. 33.

2. Lancelot Law Whyte, *The Unconscious before Freud*, p. 71.

3. Jung, vol. 8: *The Structure and Dynamics of the Psyche*, p. 292.

4. Edward C. Whitmont, *The Symbolic Quest*, p. 285.

5. Proclus, *Commentary on Timaeus*, 83.265, as quoted in Edinger, *Ego and Archetype*, p. 179.

6. See Poe, *Complete Works*, 16:186, 187, 199 for similar uses of cognate words.

7. Jung, vol. 7: *Two Essays*, p. 240.

8. Ibid.

9. This note is accurately transcribed in Poe, *Complete Works*, 16:336.

10. William James, *Some Problems of Philosophy*, pp. 115–16.

11. Jung, vol. 9, pt. 2: *Aion*, pp. 31, 34.

12. William James, *The Varieties of Religious Experience*, pp. 512–13.

13. Jung, vol. 11: *Psychology and Religion*, p. 265.

14. R. A. Yoder, *Emerson and the Orphic Poet in America*, p. xi.

15. Abrams, *Natural Supernaturalism*, p. 37.

16. Frye, *English Romanticism*, pp. 17–18.

17. Bronson Alcott, journal for 1836, as quoted in Odell Shepard, *Pedlar's Progress*, p. 149.

18. Erich Neumann, *Art and the Creative Unconscious*, p. 172.

19. Ibid., pp. 173, 177.

20. Henri F. Ellenberger, *The Discovery of the Unconscious*, p. 657.

21. See T. David Brent, "Jung's Debt to Kant," for an extensive treatment of the relations between the two thinkers, and Stephanie de Voogd, "C. G. Jung," for a more concise and informal discussion. Jung's own comments in *Memories, Dreams, Reflections*, pp. 70–74, are significant.

22. Jung, vol. 8: *Structure and Dynamics*, p. 367.

23. Ellenberger, *The Discovery of the Unconscious*, pp. 728–29.

24. Carl Gustav Carus, *Psyche*, p. 66. See James Hillman, "An Introductory Note," pp. i–viii, for more on the relations between Carus and Jung.

25. Jung, vol. 14: *Mysterium Coniunctionis*, p. 554.

26. Ellenberger, *The Discovery of the Unconscious*, p. 730.

27. James Hillman, *Re-Visioning Psychology*, p. xi.

28. A useful pioneering book is Denis Saurat, *Literature and Occult Tradition*, but clearest in outlining the basic tenets of this matrix and their relevance to literature is John Senior, *The Way Down and Out*. Also helpful are Désirée Hirst, *Hidden Riches*; Frances A. Yates, *Giordano Bruno and the Hermetic Tradition*; Wayne Shumaker, *The Occult Sciences in the Renaissance*; Luanne Frank, ed., *Literature and the Occult*; and Anya Taylor, *Magic and English Romanticism*. Kathleen Raine, *Blake and Tradition*, and F. A. C. Wilson, *W. B. Yeats and Tradition*, are among the most wide-ranging of the studies of individual authors.

29. In June K. Singer, *The Unholy Bible*, p. xvi. Singer's book itself, though containing useful insights, is not much broader in its general perspective than Harding's introduction. A more recent book applying Jungian psychology to Blake's work, Christine Gallant's *Blake and the Assimilation of Chaos*, does observe in passing that "the methodological assumptions of the two are similar, and the neo-Romantic psychologist may provide insights into the Romantic poet in a truly heuristic way" (p. 8), but does not make use of this insight in the analysis itself or elaborate it further. By contrast, Gerda S. Norvig's "Images of Wonder" effectively incorporates the subtle interrelationships between Blake and Jung.

30. Raine, *Blake and Tradition*, 1:xxvii.

31. Samuel Taylor Coleridge, *Biographia Literaria*, 1:180.

32. John S. Harrison, in *The Teachers of Emerson,* first developed and perhaps overstated the influence of the Neoplatonists on Emerson. See also Stuart Gerry Brown, "Emerson's Platonism," pp. 325–45, and Stanley Brodwin, "Emerson's Version of Plotinus," pp. 465–83. For Neoplatonic influences on Romanticism in general, see especially Frank B. Evans, "The Background of the Romantic Revival of Platonism," and George Mills Harper, *The Neoplatonism of William Blake.*

33. Abrams, *Natural Supernaturalism,* p. 169.

34. See George Mills Harper, "Thomas Taylor in America," pp. 50–51.

35. For the influence of Taylor on Emerson and Alcott, see especially Harper, "Thomas Taylor in America," pp. 49–71, and Richardson, *Myth and Literature,* pp. 50, 54–57.

36. Hillman, *Re-Visioning Psychology,* p. 198.

37. Bronson Alcott, *The Journals of Bronson Alcott,* 1:35.

38. Ibid., 1:35 n.

39. T. David Brent, personal correspondence, 1978.

40. Mircea Eliade, *The Two and the One,* p. 122.

41. Jung, vol. 8: *Structure and Dynamics,* p. 101.

42. Jung, vol. 7: *Two Essays,* p. 71.

43. Emerson, *JMN,* 3:304.

44. This reading is similar to that of Charles R. Anderson in *Emily Dickinson's Poetry,* p. 265: "The mind's perceptions of reality, both spiritual and natural, are symbols; like the poet's words ('Syllable') they stand for the truths ('Sound') that can be grasped by it from outside."

45. Emily Dickinson, *The Letters of Emily Dickinson,* 3:926.

46. Nathaniel Hawthorne, *The American Notebooks,* p. 237.

47. Northrop Frye, "The Drunken Boat," p. 16.

48. Herman Melville, *Moby-Dick,* p. 323.

49. Ibid., p. 324.

50. Ibid., p. 326.

51. Ibid.

52. Hugo McPherson, *Hawthorne as Myth-Maker,* pp. 107–28.

53. Nathaniel Hawthorne, *The Scarlet Letter,* p. 256.

54. Melville, *Moby-Dick,* p. 470.

55. Herman Melville, *Selected Poems of Herman Melville,* p. 144.

IV. Animatopoeia: Sirens of the Self

1. William Wordsworth, Preface to *The Excursion*, as quoted in Abrams, *Natural Supernaturalism*, p. 467.
2. See especially Abrams, *Natural Supernaturalism*, pp. 37–46.
3. A. J. L. Busst, "The Image of the Androgyne in the Nineteenth Century," p. 36.
4. Margaret Fuller, *Woman in the Nineteenth Century*, pp. 115–16.
5. For discussions of the subtle sexism to which this distinction sometimes leads, see Naomi R. Goldenberg, "A Feminist Critique of Jung," pp. 443–49, and D. A. Harris, Review of *Androgyny* by June Singer, pp. 783–84.
6. Maurice Barrès, *Sous l'oeil des barbares*, as quoted in Gaston Bachelard, *The Poetics of Reverie*, p. 94.
7. Neumann, *The Great Mother*, pp. 24–38. Before proceeding with our analysis, we should note that of the authors examined in this study, Poe has been treated most extensively from the frameworks of Jung and Neumann. See especially Colin Martindale, "Archetype and Reality in 'The Fall of the House of Usher,'" pp. 9–11; Roberta Reeder, "'The Black Cat' as a Study in Repression," pp. 20–22; Mark M. Hennelly, Jr., "Oedipus and Orpheus in the 'Maelström,'" pp. 6–11; and Barton Levi St. Armand, "The Dragon and the Uroboros," pp. 57–71.
8. Neumann, *Origins and History*, pp. 14–16.
9. Edgar Allan Poe, *Poems*, in *Collected Works of Edgar Allan Poe*, ed. Thomas Ollive Mabbott, 3 vols. (Cambridge: Harvard University Press, 1969–78), 1:165–66.
10. Jung, vol. 9, pt. 1: *The Archetypes and the Collective Unconscious*, p. 27.
11. Simone de Beauvoir, *The Second Sex*, p. 179.
12. Thomas Taylor, *Thomas Taylor the Platonist*, pp. 140–41.
13. Ibid., p. 142.
14. Neumann, *Amor and Psyche*, p. 89.
15. Richard Wilbur, *Poe*, pp. 133–34.
16. Barrès, letter to Rachilde, as quoted in Bachelard, *Reverie*, p. 69.
17. Barrès, *Sous l'oeil*, as quoted in Bachelard, *Reverie*, p. 94.
18. See H. B. de Groot, "The Ouroboros and the Romantic Poets," pp. 553–64, for a discussion of how the symbol continued to be resonant through the early nineteenth century.
19. Neumann, *Origins and History*, p. 16.
20. Ibid., p. 17.

21. Neumann, *The Great Mother*, p. 305.

22. See Thomas Ollive Mabbott, "The Source of the Title of Poe's 'Morella,'" pp. 26–27, and Mabbott's edition of the *Collected Works*, 2:221–22. See also James W. Gargano, "Poe's 'Morella,'" pp. 259–64, for some interesting suggestions on both the name and the story.

23. See Floyd Stovall, *Edgar Poe the Poet*, p. 252.

24. Eric W. Carlson, ed., *Introduction to Poe*, p. 577.

25. "Saneness" is emended here to "sameness" for reasons cited by David Halliburton in *Edgar Allan Poe*, p. 220. See also Poe, *Collected Works*, 2:231.

26. Johann Gottlieb Fichte, *New Exposition of the Sciences of Knowledge*, p. 102.

27. C. G. Jung and C. Kerényi, *Essays on a Science of Mythology*, p. 83.

28. The poem can be found in Poe, *Complete Works*, 2:319–20.

29. Hillman, *Re-Visioning Psychology*, p. 43.

30. Ibid.

31. Jung, vol. 9, pt. 1: *Archetypes*, p. 30.

32. Ibid.

33. Ibid., p. 27.

34. Bronson Alcott, "Orphic Sayings," p. 305.

35. Jung, vol. 9, pt. 1: *Archetypes*, p. 26.

36. Melville, *Moby-Dick*, p. 14.

37. See Mabbott's notes for sources in Poe, *Collected Works*, 2:333–34.

38. Jung, vol. 9, pt. 2: *Aion*, p. 9.

39. D. H. Lawrence, *Studies in Classic American Literature*, p. 65.

V. The Double Consciousness Revisited

1. For an extensive discussion of the convergences between Emerson and Jung, especially as related to the process of artistic creation, see Gloria Young, "'The Fountainhead of All Forms,'" pp. 241–67. Although Hyatt H. Waggoner, in *Emerson as Poet*, avoids psychological dimensions, he does note the tradition of paradoxy that Emerson and Jung share (pp. 70–74).

2. This parable can be found in Jung, vol. 9, pt. 1: *Archetypes*, pp. 129–30.

3. Jung, vol. 16: *The Practice of Psychotherapy*, p. 200.

4. As quoted in Richard Garnett, *Life of Ralph Waldo Emerson*, pp. 67–68.

5. Emerson, *JMN*, 8:10.

6. See especially Joel Porte, "Emerson, Thoreau, and the Double Consciousness," pp. 40–50, and Harold Kaplan, *Democratic Humanism and American Literature*, pp. 49–78.

7. Although Gay Wilson Allen's "Emerson and the Unconscious," pp. 26–30, does not adopt a strictly Jungian framework, it also aligns Emerson's "Soul" with the unconscious and makes several insightful observations about Emerson's psychology.

8. Stephen E. Whicher, *Freedom and Fate*, pp. 21, 22.

9. The clearest and most extensive exposition of the term in Jungian thought is Edinger, *Ego and Archetype*, pp. 37–61.

10. Emerson, *JMN*, 5:337.

11. See Edinger, *Ego and Archetype*, pp. 3–36.

12. Aside from the famous Christopher Cranch cartoon of a large eyeball on spindly legs, see, for example, Jonathan Bishop's critique in *Emerson on the Soul*, p. 15.

13. Edinger, *Ego and Archetype*, p. 5.

14. Thomas Weiskel, *The Romantic Sublime*, p. 83.

15. Whitmont, *The Symbolic Quest*, p. 309.

16. James M. Cox, "R. W. Emerson," p. 69.

17. Bloom calls "Experience" Emerson's "greatest essay" (*Figures*, p. 73), and Joel Porte calls it his "most moving" (*Representative Man*, p. 179).

18. Joseph Chiari uses these words to describe the essence of *symbolisme* in *Symbolisme from Poe to Mallarmé*, p. 37.

19. See, for example, Whicher, *Freedom and Fate*, pp. 111–19.

20. Henry D. Thoreau, *Walden*, p. 98.

VI. Words Out of the Sea: Walt Whitman

1. Walt Whitman, *The Uncollected Poetry and Prose of Walt Whitman*, 2:66.

2. See Floyd Stovall, *The Foreground of "Leaves of Grass,"* pp. 153–56, 184–204; Esther Shephard, "Possible Sources of Some of Whitman's Ideas and Symbols in *Hermes Mercurius Trismegistus* and Other Works," pp. 60–81; and George L. Sixbey, "Chanting the Square Deific—A Study in Whitman's Religion," pp. 171–95.

3. Stovall notes Whitman's interest in William Fishbough, *The Macrocosm and Microcosm*, and Andrew Jackson Davis, *The Great Harmonia*,

both of which combine occult, illuminist, scientific, and pseudoscientific ideas. From the latter, Stovall quotes the following as a possible influence on "Chanting the Square Deific": "If there exists an Evil principle, would not that principle be an integral element in the constitution of the Divine Mind?" (*The Foreground*, p. 155). Shephard in "Possible Sources" suggests that the hermetic influences on Whitman came primarily from George Sand's novel *The Countess of Rudolstadt* and cites a passage where the Divine Tetrade is invoked (p. 63).

4. Horace Traubel, *With Walt Whitman in Camden*, 1:156, as quoted in Whitman, *Leaves of Grass*, p. 442 n.

5. This analysis is developed most extensively in "A Psychological Approach to the Dogma of the Trinity," Jung, vol. 11: *Psychology and Religion*, pp. 107–200.

6. Jung, vol. 13: *Alchemical Studies*, p. 239.

7. See especially Jung, vol. 9, pt. 1: *Archetypes*, pp. 165–67. Neumann presents a detailed composite analysis of the hero myth in *Origins and History*, pp. 131–91.

8. Jung, vol. 9, pt. 1: *Archetypes*, p. 167.

9. Jung, vol. 11: *Psychology and Religion*, p. 173.

10. Ibid., p. 178.

11. Ibid., p. 176.

12. Ibid., p. 175.

13. In vol. 9, pt. 2: *Aion*, Jung writes: "Experience shows that individual mandalas are symbols of *order*, and that they occur in patients principally during times of psychic disorientation or re-orientation. As magic circles they bind and subdue the lawless powers belonging to the world of darkness, and depict or create an order that transforms the chaos into a cosmos" (pp. 31–32).

14. Harry James Cook, "The Individuation of a Poet," p. 102. Despite its too neat identification of poetic and personal processes, this is the most extensive and intelligent article on Whitman from a Jungian perspective. Ray Benoit, "The Mind's Return," pp. 21–28, draws some interesting relations but avoids specific analysis of the poetry.

15. Cook, "Individuation," p. 103.

16. Hillman, *Re-Visioning Psychology*, p. 33.

17. James Hillman, *The Dream and the Underworld*, p. 54.

18. Hillman, *Re-Visioning Psychology*, p. 35.

19. The autoerotic qualities of the poem are stressed in Stephen A. Black's psychoanalytic reading in *Whitman's Journeys into Chaos*, pp. 125–37. An earlier Freudian reading of the poem, Edwin H. Miller's

Walt Whitman's Poetry, pp. 72–84, views the poem in terms of a sexual rite of passage and provides a more sensitive and detailed reading than that of Black.

20. Georges Bataille, *Death and Sensuality*, p. 11.

21. Waskow makes a similar point about this line in his detailed analysis of the poem (*Whitman*, p. 146).

22. Mutlu Blasing, " 'The Sleepers,' " p. 116.

23. John Dryden, *On the Dramatique Poetry of the Last Age*, as quoted in John Boe, "To Kill Mercutio," p. 97. Boe's article is a provocative Jungian analysis of Shakespeare's development.

24. Hillman, *Re-Visioning Psychology*, p. 42.

25. Jung, vol. 10: *Civilization in Transition*, p. 149.

26. See especially Miller, *Walt Whitman's Poetry*, p. 178.

27. From the 1860 version, as reprinted in R. W. B. Lewis, ed., *The Presence of Walt Whitman*, p. 192.

28. Neumann, *Origins and History*, p. 14.

29. Louise J. Kaplan, *Oneness and Separateness*, p. 32.

30. Hawthorne, *The Scarlet Letter*, pp. 3–4.

31. Richard Chase, " 'Out of the Cradle' as a Romance," pp. 52–71.

32. Neumann, *Origins and History*, p. 17.

VII. Kora in Heaven: Emily Dickinson

1. The most important recent study is Richard B. Sewall, *The Life of Emily Dickinson*. Barton Levi St. Armand's forthcoming *The Soul's Society* also promises to be a valuable source of biographical and historical information.

2. Although the situation has changed somewhat since the appearance of his article, George Monteiro's "The One and Many Emily Dickinsons," pp. 137–41, provides a concise analysis of the dilemmas of Dickinson criticism.

3. Albert Gelpi, in *The Tenth Muse*, pp. 219–99, and in "Emily Dickinson and the Deerslayer," pp. 122–34, uses a similar strategy in some parts of his treatment and reaches similar conclusions about the nature of the masculine lover and the relations to the Persephone myth. Although this chapter has benefited significantly from Gelpi's work, the main lines of analysis were worked out independently and delivered as a public lecture at the University of Colorado before Gelpi's book appeared. Frederick L. Morey has also applied Jungian and archetypal criticism in

"The Four Fundamental Archetypes in Mythology, as Exemplified in Emily Dickinson's Poems," pp. 196–206, and in "Hundred Best Poems of Emily Dickinson," pp. 4–72.

4. Thomas H. Johnson, *Emily Dickinson*, pp. 98–99.

5. Ruth Miller, *The Poetry of Emily Dickinson*, pp. 91, 92.

6. Ibid., p. 92.

7. Gelpi, *The Tenth Muse*, p. 242.

8. See ibid., pp. 199–201.

9. R. P. Blackmur, "Emily Dickinson's Notation," p. 231.

10. Johnson, *Emily Dickinson*, p. 237.

11. Clark Griffith, *The Long Shadow*, p. 173.

12. *In Praise of Krishna*, p. 66.

13. W. B. Yeats, *Essays and Introductions*, p. 393.

14. Jung and Kerényi, *A Science of Mythology*, p. 109.

15. Dickinson, *Letters*, 2:463.

16. Jung, vol. 7: *Two Essays*, p. 191.

17. Rosemary Gordon, "The Death Instinct and Its Relation to the Self," pp. 119–33.

18. Ibid., pp. 120–21.

19. Ibid., p. 124.

20. Jung, vol. 5: *Symbols of Transformation*, p. 285.

21. Dickinson, *Letters*, 3:798.

22. Gordon, "The Death Instinct," pp. 131–32.

23. Bataille, *Death and Sensuality*, pp. 11–12.

24. Gaston Bachelard, *The Psychoanalysis of Fire*, p. 16.

25. Neumann, *Origins and History*, p. 12.

26. Gordon, "Symbols," p. 298.

27. David C. McClelland, *The Roots of Consciousness*, p. 183.

28. Ellen Greenberger, "Fantasies of Women Confronting Death," pp. 252–60.

29. Ellen Greenberger, " 'Flirting' with Death," p. 197.

30. Ibid., p. 200.

31. Joseph L. Henderson and Maud Oakes, *The Wisdom of the Serpent*.

32. *The Homeric Hymns*, pp. 91–93.

33. Ibid., p. 126.

34. "The Eleusinia," p. 298.

35. See, for example, poems 280, 341, and 943 in the Johnson edition.

36. Dickinson, *Letters*, 1:104.

37. Gelpi, *The Tenth Muse*, p. 249.

38. McClelland, *The Roots of Consciousness*, pp. 191–92.

39. Pindar, *Carmina cum Fragmentis*, fragment 121.

40. Jung and Kerényi, *A Science of Mythology*, p. 162.

41. "The Eleusinia," p. 303.

42. Griffith, *The Long Shadow*, p. 93.

43. Henderson and Oakes, *The Wisdom of the Serpent*, p. 59.

Afterword

1. Thoreau, *Walden*, p. 321.

2. Marie Bonaparte, *Edgar Poe*, as quoted in Eric W. Carlson, ed., *The Recognition of Edgar Allan Poe*, p. 175.

3. See Frederick Crews, *The Sins of the Fathers*, especially pp. 44–60, 80–95.

4. See Black, *Whitman's Journeys into Chaos*, especially pp. 50–54.

5. Jung, vol. 11: *Psychology and Religion*, p. 149 n. For a clear and sympathetic account of Jung's concept of the archetype, see Jacobi, *Complex/Archetype/Symbol*, pp. 31–73.

BIBLIOGRAPHY

Abrams, M. H. *Natural Supernaturalism: Tradition and Revolution in Romantic Literature*. New York: W. W. Norton Co., 1971.

Alcott, Bronson. *The Journals of Bronson Alcott*. Edited by Odell Shepard. 2 vols. 1938. Reprint. Port Washington, N. Y.: Kennikat Press, 1966.

――――. "Orphic Sayings." *Dial* 1 (1840): 85–98. Reprinted in Perry Miller, *The Transcendentalists: An Anthology*. Cambridge: Harvard University Press, 1950.

Allen, Gay Wilson. "Emerson and the Unconscious." *ATQ: The American Transcendental Quarterly* 19 (1973): 26–30.

Anderson, Charles R. *Emily Dickinson's Poetry: Stairway of Surprise*. New York: Holt, Rinehart & Winston, 1960.

Bachelard, Gaston. *The Poetics of Reverie: Childhood, Language, and the Cosmos*. Translated by Daniel Russell. Boston: Beacon Press, 1969.

――――. *The Psychoanalysis of Fire*. Translated by Alan C. M. Ross. Boston: Beacon Press, 1964.

Baird, James. *Ishmael*. Baltimore: Johns Hopkins Press, 1956.

Bataille, Georges. *Death and Sensuality: A Study of Eroticism and the Taboo*. 1962. Reprint. New York: Ballantine Books, 1969.

Beauvoir, Simone de. *The Second Sex*. Translated by H. M. Parshley. New York: Alfred A. Knopf, 1953.

Beebe, Maurice. "The Universe of Roderick Usher." *Personalist* 37 (1956): 147–60.

Bibliography

Bennet, E. A. *C. G. Jung*. New York: E. P. Dutton & Co., 1962.

Benoit, Ray. "'The Mind's Return: Whitman, Teilhard, and Jung." *Walt Whitman Review* 13 (1967): 21–28.

Bishop, Jonathan. *Emerson on the Soul*. Cambridge: Harvard University Press, 1964.

Black, Stephen A. *Whitman's Journeys into Chaos: A Psychoanalytic Study of the Poetic Process*. Princeton: Princeton University Press, 1975.

Blackmur, R. P. "Emily Dickinson's Notation." *Kenyon Review* 18 (1956): 224–37.

Blasing, Mutlu. "'The Sleepers': The Problem of the Self in Whitman." *Walt Whitman Review* 21 (1975): 111–19.

Bloom, Harold. *Figures of Capable Imagination*. New York: Seabury Press, 1976.

Boe, John. "To Kill Mercutio: Thoughts on Shakespeare's Psychological Development." *Quadrant* 8 (1975): 97–105.

Bonaparte, Marie. *Edgar Poe: Etude psychoanalytique*. 2 vols. Paris: Denoël et Stelle, 1933. Translated as *The Life and Works of Edgar Allan Poe* by John Rodker. London: Imago, 1949.

Brent, T. David. "Jung's Debt to Kant: The Transcendental Method and the Structure of Jung's Psychology." Ph.D. dissertation, University of Chicago, 1977.

Brodwin, Stanley. "Emerson's Version of Plotinus: The Flight to Beauty." *Journal of the History of Ideas* 35 (1974): 465–83.

Brown, Stuart Gerry. "Emerson's Platonism." *New England Quarterly* 18 (1945): 325–45.

Bushnell, Horace. "Preliminary Dissertation on the Nature of Language, as Related to Thought and Spirit." In *Horace Bushnell*, edited by H. Shelton Smith. New York: Oxford University Press, 1965.

Busst, A. J. L. "The Image of the Androgyne in the Nineteenth Century." In *Romantic Mythologies*, edited by Ian Fletcher. London: Routledge & Kegan Paul, 1967.

Carlson, Eric W. *Poe on the Soul of Man*. Baltimore: Edgar Allan Poe Society, 1973.

———, ed. *Introduction to Poe: A Thematic Reader*. Glenview, Ill.: Scott Foresman, 1967.

———, ed. *The Recognition of Edgar Allan Poe*. Ann Arbor: University of Michigan Press, 1966.

Carpenter, Frederic Ives. *Emerson and Asia*. Cambridge: Harvard University Press, 1930.

Bibliography

Carus, Carl Gustav. *Psyche: On the Development of the Soul.* Translated by Renata Welch. 1846. Reprint. New York: Spring Publications, 1970.

Chase, Richard. "'Out of the Cradle' as a Romance." In *The Presence of Walt Whitman: Selected Papers from the English Institute,* edited by R. W. B. Lewis. New York: Columbia University Press, 1962.

Chiari, Joseph. *Symbolisme from Poe to Mallarmé.* 2d ed. New York: Gordian Press, 1970.

Christy, Arthur E. *The Orient in American Transcendentalism: A Study of Emerson, Thoreau, and Alcott.* New York: Columbia University Press, 1932.

Colacurcio, Michael J. "The Symbolic and the Symptomatic: D. H. Lawrence in Recent American Criticism." *American Quarterly* 27 (1975): 486–501.

Coleridge, Samuel Taylor. *Biographia Literaria.* Edited by J. Shawcross. 2 vols. London: Oxford University Press, 1907.

Cook, Harry James. "The Individuation of a Poet: The Process of Becoming in Whitman's 'The Sleepers.'" *Walt Whitman Review* 21 (1975): 101–10.

Coulter, James A. *The Literary Microcosm: Theories of Interpretation of the Later Neoplatonists.* Leiden: E. J. Brill, 1976.

Cox, James M. "R. W. Emerson: The Circles of the Eye." In *Emerson: Prophecy, Metamorphosis, and Influence; Selected Papers from the English Institute,* edited by David Levin. New York: Columbia University Press, 1975.

Crews, Frederick. *Out of My System: Psychoanalysis, Ideology, and Critical Method.* New York: Oxford University Press, 1975.

————. *The Sins of the Fathers: Hawthorne's Psychological Themes.* New York: Oxford University Press, 1966.

Dickinson, Emily. *The Letters of Emily Dickinson.* Edited by Thomas H. Johnson and Theodora Ward. 3 vols. Cambridge: Harvard University Press, 1958.

————. *The Poems of Emily Dickinson, Including Variant Readings Critically Compared with All Known Manuscripts.* Edited by Thomas H. Johnson. 3 vols. Cambridge: Harvard University Press, 1955.

Duncan, Jeffrey L. *The Power and Form of Emerson's Thought.* Charlottesville: University Press of Virginia, 1973.

Edinger, Edward F. *Ego and Archetype: Individuation and the Religious Function of the Psyche.* New York: Putnam, 1972.

Bibliography

————. *Melville's Moby-Dick: A Jungian Commentary.* New York: New Directions, 1978.

"The Eleusinia." *Atlantic Monthly* 4 (1859): 295–303.

Eliade, Mircea. *The Two and the One.* Translated by J. M. Cohen. New York: Harper & Row, 1965.

Ellenberger, Henri F. *The Discovery of the Unconscious: The History and Evolution of Dynamic Psychiatry.* New York: Basic Books, 1970.

Emerson, Ralph Waldo. *The Complete Works of Ralph Waldo Emerson.* Edited by Edward Waldo Emerson. Centenary Edition. 12 vols. Boston and New York: Houghton Mifflin, 1903–4.

————. *The Journals and Miscellaneous Notebooks of Ralph Waldo Emerson.* Edited by William H. Gilman, Alfred R. Ferguson, George P. Clark, Merrell R. Davis, Merton M. Sealts, Harrison Hayford, Ralph H. Orth, J. E. Parsons, A. W. Plumstead, Linda Allardt, and Susan Sutton Smith. 14 vols. Cambridge: Harvard University Press, 1960–.

Evans, Frank B. "The Background of the Romantic Revival of Platonism." Ph.D. dissertation, Princeton University, 1938.

Feidelson, Charles, Jr. *Symbolism and American Literature.* Chicago: University of Chicago Press, 1953.

Feldman, Burton, and Richardson, Robert D., Jr. *The Rise of Modern Mythology, 1680–1860.* Bloomington: Indiana University Press, 1972.

Fichte, Johann Gottlieb. *New Exposition of the Sciences of Knowledge.* Translated by A. E. O. Kioeger. St. Louis: Philosophical Library, 1869.

Fiedler, Leslie A. *Love and Death in the American Novel.* Rev. ed. New York: Stein & Day, 1966.

Frank, Luanne, ed. *Literature and the Occult: Essays in Comparative Literature.* Arlington: University of Texas at Arlington Publications, 1977.

Franklin, H. Bruce. *Future Perfect: American Science Fiction of the Nineteenth Century.* Rev. ed. New York: Oxford University Press, 1978.

Frye, Northrop. "The Drunken Boat: The Revolutionary Element in Romanticism." In *Romanticism Reconsidered: Selected Papers from the English Institute.* New York: Columbia University Press, 1963.

————. *Spiritus Mundi: Essays on Literature, Myth, and Society.* Bloomington: Indiana University Press, 1976.

Bibliography

_____. *A Study of English Romanticism.* New York: Random House, 1968.

Fuller, Margaret. *Woman in the Nineteenth Century.* 1845. Reprint. New York: W. W. Norton Co., 1971.

Gallant, Christine. *Blake and the Assimilation of Chaos.* Princeton: Princeton University Press, 1978.

Gargano, James W. "Poe's 'Morella': A Note on Her Name." *American Literature* 47 (1975): 259–64.

Garnett, Richard. *Life of Ralph Waldo Emerson.* London: Walter Scott, 1888.

Gelpi, Albert. "Emily Dickinson and the Deerslayer: The Dilemma of the Woman Poet in America." In *Shakespeare's Sisters: Feminist Essays on Woman Poets*, edited by Sandra M. Gilbert and Susan Gubar. Bloomington: Indiana University Press, 1979.

_____. *The Tenth Muse: The Psyche of the American Poet.* Cambridge: Harvard University Press, 1975.

Goldenberg, Naomi R. "A Feminist Critique of Jung." *Signs: Journal of Women in Culture and Society* 2 (1976): 443–49.

Golding, Alan C. "Reductive and Expansive Language: Semantic Strategies in *Eureka.*" *Poe Studies* 11 (1978): 1–5.

Gordon, Rosemary. "The Death Instinct and Its Relation to the Self." *Journal of Analytical Psychology* 6 (1961): 119–33.

_____. "Symbols: Content and Process." In *The Reality of the Psyche: The Proceedings of the Third International Congress for Analytical Psychology*, edited by Joseph B. Wheelwright. London: Barrie & Rockliff, 1968.

Greenberger, Ellen. "Fantasies of Women Confronting Death." *Journal of Consulting Psychology* 29 (1965): 252–60.

_____. "'Flirting' with Death: Fantasies of a Critically Ill Woman." *Journal of Projective Techniques and Personality Assessment* 30 (1966): 197–204.

Griffith, Clark. *The Long Shadow: Emily Dickinson's Tragic Poetry.* Princeton: Princeton University Press, 1964.

Groot, H. B. de. "The Ouroboros and the Romantic Poets: A Renaissance Emblem in Blake, Coleridge, and Shelley." *English Studies* 50 (1969): 553–64.

Halliburton, David. *Edgar Allan Poe: A Phenomenological View.* Princeton: Princeton University Press, 1973.

Harper, George Mills. *The Neoplatonism of William Blake.* Chapel Hill:

Bibliography

The University of North Carolina Press, 1961.

————. "Thomas Taylor in America," In *Thomas Taylor the Platonist*, edited, with introductions, by Kathleen Raine and George Mills Harper. Princeton: Princeton University Press, 1969 (Bollingen Series LXXXVIII).

Harris, D. A. Review of *Androgyny: Toward a New Theory of Sexuality* by June Singer. *Signs: Journal of Women in Culture and Society* 4 (1979): 783–84.

Harrison, John S. *The Teachers of Emerson*. New York: Sturgis & Wallace, 1910.

Hawthorne, Nathaniel. *The American Notebooks*. Edited by Claude M. Simpson. Centenary Edition. Columbus: Ohio State University Press, 1972.

————. *The House of the Seven Gables*. Centenary Edition. Columbus: Ohio State University Press, 1965.

————. *Mosses from an Old Manse*. Centenary Edition. Columbus: Ohio State University Press, 1974.

————. *The Scarlet Letter*. Centenary Edition. Columbus: Ohio State University Press, 1962.

Henderson, Joseph L., and Oakes, Maud. *The Wisdom of the Serpent: The Myths of Death, Rebirth, and Resurrection*. New York: George Braziller, 1963.

Hennelly, Mark M., Jr. "Oedipus and Orpheus in the 'Maelström': The Traumatic Rebirth of the Artist." *Poe Studies* 9 (1976): 6–11.

Hillman, James. *The Dream and the Underworld*. New York: Harper & Row, 1979.

————. "An Introductory Note." In Carl Gustav Carus, *Psyche: On the Development of the Soul*. Translated by Renata Welch. 1846. Reprint. New York: Spring Publications, 1970.

————. *Re-Visioning Psychology*. New York: Harper & Row, 1975.

Hirsch, E. D. *Validity in Interpretation*. New Haven: Yale University Press, 1967.

Hirst, Désirée. *Hidden Riches: Traditional Symbolism from the Renaissance to Blakę*. London: Eyre & Spottiswoode, 1964.

Hoffman, Daniel. *Poe Poe Poe Poe Poe Poe Poe*. Garden City, N.Y.: Doubleday, 1972.

The Homeric Hymns. Translated by Charles Boer. Chicago: Swallow Press, 1970.

In Praise of Krishna: Songs from the Bengali. Translated by Edward C.

Bibliography

Dimock, Jr., and Denise Levertov. Garden City, N.Y.: Doubleday, 1967.

Jacobi, Jolande. *Complex/Archetype/Symbol in the Psychology of C. G. Jung.* Translated by Ralph Manheim. Princeton: Princeton University Press, 1959 (Bollingen Series LVII).

James, William. *Some Problems of Philosophy: A Beginning of an Introduction to Philosophy.* London: Longmans, Green, & Co., 1911.

_____. *The Varieties of Religious Experience: A Study in Human Nature.* London: Longmans, Green, & Co., 1902.

Johnson, Thomas H. *Emily Dickinson: An Interpretative Biography.* Cambridge: Harvard University Press, 1955.

Jung, C. G. *Collected Works.* Edited by Herbert Read, Michael Fordham, Gerhard Adler, and William McGuire. Translated by R. F. C. Hull. 18 vols. 2d ed. Princeton: Princeton University Press, 1967–79 (Bollingen Series XX).

Vol. 5. *Symbols of Transformation.* 1967.

Vol. 6. *Psychological Types.* 1971.

Vol. 7. *Two Essays on Analytical Psychology.* 1966.

Vol. 8. *The Structure and Dynamics of the Psyche.* 1969.

Vol. 9, pt. 1. *The Archetypes and the Collective Unconscious.* 1968.

Vol. 9, pt. 2. *Aion: Researches into the Phenomenology of the Self.* 1968.

Vol. 10. *Civilization in Transition.* 1970.

Vol. 11. *Psychology and Religion: West and East.* 1969.

Vol. 13. *Alchemical Studies.* 1967.

Vol. 14. *Mysterium Coniunctionis.* 1970.

Vol. 15. *The Spirit in Man, Art, and Literature.* 1966.

Vol. 16. *The Practice of Psychotherapy.* 1966.

_____. *Memories, Dreams, Reflections.* Edited by Aniela Jaffé. Translated by Richard and Clara Winston. Rev. ed. New York: Random House, 1961.

_____, and Carl Kerényi. *Essays on a Science of Mythology: The Myth of the Divine Child and the Mysteries of Eleusis.* Translated by R. F. C. Hull. Rev. ed. Princeton: Princeton University Press, 1963 (Bollingen Series XXII).

Kaplan, Harold. *Democratic Humanism and American Literature.* Chicago: University of Chicago Press, 1972.

Kaplan, Louise J. *Oneness and Separateness: From Infant to Individual.* New York: Simon & Schuster, 1978.

Bibliography

Kuklick, Bruce. "Myth and Symbol in American Studies." *American Quarterly* 24 (1972): 435–50.

Lawrence, D. H. *Studies in Classic American Literature.* 1923. Reprint. New York: Viking Press, 1961.

Lewis, R. W. B. *The American Adam: Innocence, Tragedy and Tradition in the Nineteenth Century.* Chicago: University of Chicago Press, 1955.

———, ed. *The Presence of Walt Whitman: Selected Papers from the English Institute.* New York: Columbia University Press, 1962.

Lynen, John F. *The Design of the Present: Essays on Time and Form in American Literature.* New Haven: Yale University Press, 1969.

Mabbott, Thomas Ollive. "The Source of the Title of Poe's 'Morella.'" *Notes and Queries* 172 (1937): 26–27.

McClelland, David C. *The Roots of Consciousness.* Princeton: Van Nostrand, 1964.

McPherson, Hugo. *Hawthorne as Myth-Maker: A Study in Imagination.* Toronto: University of Toronto Press, 1969.

Martindale, Colin. "Archetype and Reality in 'The Fall of the House of Usher.'" *Poe Studies* 5 (1972): 9–11.

Marx, Leo. "American Studies—A Defense of an Unscientific Method." *New Literary History* 1 (1969): 75–90.

———. *The Machine in the Garden: Technology and the Pastoral Ideal in America.* New York: Oxford University Press, 1964.

Matthiessen, F. O. *American Renaissance: Art and Expression in the Age of Emerson and Whitman.* New York: Oxford University Press, 1941.

Melville, Herman. *Mardi, and a Voyage Thither.* Edited by Harrison Hayford, Hershel Parker, and G. Thomas Tanselle. Evanston: Northwestern University Press, 1970.

———. *Moby-Dick; or, The Whale.* Edited by Harrison Hayford and Hershel Parker. New York: W. W. Norton Co., 1967.

———. *Selected Poems of Herman Melville.* Edited by Hennig Cohen. Carbondale: Southern Illinois University Press, 1964.

Miller, Edwin H. *Walt Whitman's Poetry: A Psychological Journey.* Boston: Houghton Mifflin, 1968.

Miller, Perry. *The Transcendentalists: An Anthology.* Cambridge: Harvard University Press, 1950.

Miller, Ruth. *The Poetry of Emily Dickinson.* Middletown, Conn.: Wesleyan University Press, 1968.

Monteiro, George. "The One and Many Emily Dickinsons." *American Literary Realism, 1870–1910* 7 (1974): 137–41.

Bibliography

Morey, Frederick L. "The Four Fundamental Archetypes in Mythology, as Exemplified in Emily Dickinson's Poems." *Emily Dickinson Bulletin* 24 (1973): 196–206.

——. "Hundred Best Poems of Emily Dickinson." *Emily Dickinson Bulletin* 27 (1975): 4–72.

Neumann, Erich. *Amor and Psyche: The Psychic Development of the Feminine.* Translated by Ralph Manheim. Princeton: Princeton University Press, 1956 (Bollingen Series LIV).

——. *Art and the Creative Unconscious: Four Essays.* Translated by Ralph Manheim. Princeton: Princeton University Press, 1959 (Bollingen Series LXI).

——. *The Great Mother: An Analysis of the Archetype.* Translated by Ralph Manheim. 2d ed. Princeton: Princeton University Press, 1963 (Bollingen Series XLVII).

——. *The Origins and History of Consciousness.* Translated by R. F. C. Hull. Princeton: Princeton University Press, 1954 (Bollingen Series XLII).

Norvig, Gerda S. "Images of Wonder, Images of Truth: Blake's Illustrations to *The Pilgrim's Progress.*" Ph.D. dissertation, Brandeis University, 1978.

Pindar. *Carmina cum Fragmentis.* Edited by Cecil Maurice Bowra. Oxford: Oxford Classical Texts, 1947.

Poe, Edgar Allan. *Collected Works of Edgar Allan Poe.* Edited by Thomas Ollive Mabbott. 3 vols. Cambridge: Harvard University Press, 1969–78.

——. *The Complete Works of Edgar Allan Poe.* Edited by James A. Harrison. 17 vols. 1902. Reprint. New York: AMS Press, 1965.

Porte, Joel. "Emerson, Thoreau, and the Double Consciousness." *New England Quarterly* 41 (1968): 40–50.

——. *Representative Man: Ralph Waldo Emerson in His Time.* New York: Oxford University Press, 1979.

Porter, David. *Emerson and Literary Change.* Cambridge: Harvard University Press, 1978.

Raine, Kathleen. *Blake and Tradition.* 2 vols. Princeton: Princeton University Press, 1968 (Bollingen Series XXXV).

Reeder, Roberta. "'The Black Cat' as a Study in Repression." *Poe Studies* 7 (1974): 20–22.

Richardson, Robert D., Jr. *Myth and Literature in the American Renaissance.* Bloomington: Indiana University Press, 1978.

St. Armand, Barton Levi. "The Dragon and the Uroboros: Themes of

Bibliography

Metamorphosis in *Arthur Gordon Pym.*" *ATQ: The American Transcendental Quarterly* 37 (1978): 57–71.

_____. "The Mysteries of Edgar Poe: The Quest for a Monomyth in Gothic Literature." In *The Gothic Imagination: Essays in Dark Romanticism*, edited by G. R. Thompson. Pullman: Washington State University Press, 1974.

_____. "Poe's 'Sober Mystification': The Uses of Alchemy in 'The Gold Bug.'" *Poe Studies* 4 (1971): 1–7.

_____. *The Roots of Horror in the Fiction of H. P. Lovecraft.* Elizabethtown, N.Y.: Dragon Press, 1977.

_____. "Usher Unveiled: Poe and the Metaphysic of Gnosticism." *Poe Studies* 5 (1972): 1–8.

Saurat, Denis. *Literature and Occult Tradition: Studies in Philosophical Poetry.* Translated by Dorothy Bolton. 1930. Reprint. Port Washington, N.Y.: Kennikat Press, 1966.

Senior, John. *The Way Down and Out: The Occult in Symbolist Literature.* Ithaca: Cornell University Press, 1959.

Sewall, Richard B. *The Life of Emily Dickinson.* 2 vols. New York: Farrar, Straus & Giroux, 1974.

Shepard, Odell. *Pedlar's Progress: The Life of Bronson Alcott.* Boston: Little, Brown, 1937.

Shephard, Esther. "Possible Sources of Some of Whitman's Ideas and Symbols in *Hermes Mercurius Trismegistus* and Other Works." *Modern Language Quarterly* 14 (1953): 60–81.

Shumaker, Wayne. *The Occult Sciences in the Renaissance: A Study in Intellectual Patterns.* Berkeley and Los Angeles: University of California Press, 1972.

Singer, June K. *The Unholy Bible: A Psychological Interpretation of William Blake.* New York: Putnam, 1970.

Sixbey, George L. "Chanting the Square Deific—A Study in Whitman's Religion." *American Literature* 9 (1937): 171–95.

Slotkin, Richard. *Regeneration through Violence: The Mythology of the American Frontier, 1600–1860.* Middletown, Conn.: Wesleyan University Press, 1973.

Smith, Henry Nash. *Virgin Land: The American West as Symbol and Myth.* Cambridge: Harvard University Press, 1950.

Stein, Leopold. "What Is a Symbol Supposed to Be?" *Journal of Analytical Psychology* 2 (1957): 73–84.

Stovall, Floyd. *Edgar Poe the Poet: Essays New and Old on the Man and His Work.* Charlottesville: University Press of Virginia, 1969.

Bibliography

_____. *The Foreground of "Leaves of Grass."* Charlottesville: University Press of Virginia, 1974.

Taylor, Anya. *Magic and English Romanticism.* Athens: University of Georgia Press, 1979.

Taylor, Thomas. *Thomas Taylor the Platonist: Selected Writings.* Edited, with introductions, by Kathleen Raine and George Mills Harper. Princeton: Princeton University Press, 1969 (Bollingen Series LXXXVIII).

Thoreau, Henry D. *Walden.* Edited by J. Lyndon Shanley. Princeton: Princeton University Press, 1971.

_____. *A Week on the Concord and Merrimack Rivers.* Edited by Carl Hovde. Princeton: Princeton University Press, 1980.

Voogd, Stephanie de. "C. G. Jung: Psychologist of the Future, 'Philosopher' of the Past." In *Spring: An Annual of Archetypal Psychology and Jungian Thought,* edited by James Hillman. Zurich: Spring Publications, 1977.

Waggoner, Hyatt H. *American Poets from the Puritans to the Present.* Boston: Houghton Mifflin, 1968.

_____. *Emerson as Poet.* Princeton: Princeton University Press, 1974.

Waskow, Howard J. *Whitman: Explorations in Form.* Chicago: University of Chicago Press, 1966.

Weiskel, Thomas. *The Romantic Sublime: Studies in the Structure and Psychology of Transcendence.* Baltimore: The Johns Hopkins University Press, 1976.

Whicher, Stephen E. *Freedom and Fate: An Inner Life of Ralph Waldo Emerson.* Philadelphia: University of Pennsylvania Press, 1953.

Whitman, Walt. *Leaves of Grass.* Edited by Harold W. Blodgett and Sculley Bradley. Comprehensive Reader's Edition. New York: New York University Press, 1965.

_____. *Prose Works, 1892.* Edited by Floyd Stovall. 2 vols. New York: New York University Press, 1963.

_____. *The Uncollected Poetry and Prose of Walt Whitman.* Edited by Emory Holloway. 2 vols. Garden City, N.Y.: Doubleday, Page & Co., 1921.

Whitmont, Edward C. *The Symbolic Quest: Basic Concepts of Analytical Psychology.* 1969. Reprint. Princeton: Princeton University Press, 1978.

Whyte, Lancelot Law. *The Unconscious before Freud.* New York: Basic Books, 1960.

Wilbur, Richard. *Poe.* New York: Dell, 1959.

Bibliography

Wilson, F. A. C. *W. B. Yeats and Tradition.* London: V. Gollanz, 1958.

Yates, Frances A. *Giordano Bruno and the Hermetic Tradition.* London: Routledge & Kegan Paul, 1964.

Yeats, W. B. *Essays and Introductions.* New York: Macmillan, 1961.

Yoder, R. A. *Emerson and the Orphic Poet in America.* Berkeley: University of California Press, 1978.

Young, Gloria. " 'The Fountainhead of All Forms': Poetry and the Unconscious in Emerson and Howard Nemerov." In *Artful Thunder: Versions of the Romantic Tradition in American Literature in Honor of Howard P. Vincent,* edited by Robert J. DeMott and Sanford E. Marovitz. Kent, Ohio: Kent State University Press, 1975.

Zimmer, Heinrich. *The King and the Corpse: Tales of the Soul's Conquest of Evil.* Edited by Joseph Campbell. Princeton: Princeton University Press, 1956 (Bollingen Series XI).

_____. *Myths and Symbols in Indian Art and Civilization.* Edited by Joseph Campbell. Princeton: Princeton University Press, 1946 (Bollingen Series VI).

INDEX